Game AI Pro 360

Game AI Pro 360
Guide to Character Behavior

Edited by
Steve Rabin

CRC Press
Taylor & Francis Group
Boca Raton London New York

CRC Press is an imprint of the
Taylor & Francis Group, an **informa** business

CRC Press
Taylor & Francis Group
6000 Broken Sound Parkway NW, Suite 300
Boca Raton, FL 33487-2742

Printed on acid-free paper

International Standard Book Number-13: 978-0-367-15114-0 (paperback)
International Standard Book Number-13: 978-0-367-15115-7 (hardback)

Visit the Taylor & Francis Web site at
http://www.taylorandfrancis.com

and the CRC Press Web site at
http://www.crcpress.com

Contents

About the Editor

Steve Rabin has been a key figure in the game AI community for more than a decade and is currently a principal software engineer at Nintendo Technology Development. After initially working as an AI engineer at several Seattle startups, he managed and edited seven game AI books in the "Game AI Pro" series and the "AI Game Programming Wisdom" series. He also edited the book *Introduction to Game Development* and has more than two dozen articles published in the "Game Programming Gems" series. He has been an invited keynote speaker at several AI conferences, founded the AI Game Programmers Guild in 2008, and founded the GDC AI Summit where he has been a summit adviser since 2009. Steve is a principal lecturer at the DigiPen Institute of Technology, Redmond, Washington, where he has taught game AI since 2006. He earned a BS in computer engineering and an MS in computer science, both at the University of Washington, Seattle, Washington.

About the Contributors

Mark Botta has been programming in the video game industry for 20 years. He started on the Sega Genesis and has created games for the PC and almost every generation of the Sony PlayStation and Microsoft Xbox. He has worked on side-scrollers, shooters, MMORPGs, and action, stealth, and horror games, including *Tomb Raider*, *Uncharted 3*, and *The Last of Us*. He has a wide range of game programming experience but specializes in AI. He earned his BSc in computer science from the University of California, San Diego. When not programming, he's exploring Los Angeles looking for the perfect iced tea.

Phil Carlisle is a senior lecturer at the University of Bolton, Bolton, United Kingdom. He is also the owner of an indie studio called MindFlock Ltd., which he founded after over a decade in the game industry working on game characters and artificial intelligence. Phil has worked on numerous published games, primarily from the multimillion-selling *Worms* franchise.

Max Dyckhoff is an AI software engineer with 10 years of industry experience at Naughty Dog, Blizzard, Bungie, and Free Radical Design. His experience includes work on the AI of blockbuster titles such as *The Last of Us*, *Halo 3*, and *Halo Reach*. He has spoken on buddy AI, behavior trees, and knowledge representation at the Game Developers Conference and the Neural Information Processing Systems Conference. He holds a master of engineering in computer systems and software engineering from the University of York in the United Kingdom. He was born in Scotland, moved to the United States in 2006, and now lives in Santa Monica with his daughter. Currently, he is at Naughty Dog working on AI and other fun things for upcoming titles.

Sebastian Hanlon is a programmer-turned-designer who has been with BioWare Edmonton since 2006. His shipped game credits include *Dragon Age: Origins*, *Dragon Age II*, *Dragon Age: Inquisition*, *Mass Effect 2*, and *Mass Effect 3*. Sebastian holds a BSc and an MSc in computer science from the University of Lethbridge, Lethbridge, Canada.

Mike Lewis entered the game industry as a programmer in early 2002, and has spent most of the intervening years focusing on game AI and surrounding technologies. He has lectured at the Game Developers Conference and published articles in previous volumes of *Game AI Pro*. Currently, Mike calls ArenaNet, LLC, home, where he tirelessly schemes to bring better AI to the world of massively multiplayer online gaming.

John Manslow started writing games on his Vic-20 as a teenager and gradually became more and more interested in smart AI. Having completed a degree and then a PhD in the subject, he joined Codemasters as the AI specialist in their R&D team, where he worked on several projects to bring the next generation AI to Codemasters' games. Since then, John has worked for several companies outside the industry but has remained focused on AI and statistical analytics.

Michael Mateas is the codirector of Expressive Intelligence Studio and the director of the Center for Games and Playable Media at the University of California, Santa Cruz, California. His research in game AI focuses on enabling new forms of gameplay through innovative AI solutions. The Expressive Intelligence Studio has ongoing projects in autonomous characters, interactive storytelling, game design support systems, AI models of creativity, and automated game generation. With Andrew Stern, Michael created *Façade*, which uses AI techniques to combine rich autonomous characters with interactive plot control to create the world's first, fully produced, real-time, interactive drama. Michael received his PhD in computer science from Carnegie Mellon University, Pittsburgh, Pennsylvania.

Travis McIntosh has worked at Naughty Dog, Santa Monica, California, for 9 years. He was lead programmer on *Uncharted 1*, *2*, and *3*, as well as *The Last of Us*. He has personally worked on gameplay systems as diverse as player control, cameras, AI, and animation. He is a devout Christian and lives with his wonderful wife, Vivien, and their son, Corin, in El Segundo, California.

Sergio Ocio Barriales has been working in the game industry since 2005. He received his PhD in 2010 from the University of Oviedo, Asturias, Spain, with his thesis about hinted-execution behavior trees. He has worked on the AI for numerous major titles, such as *Driver San Francisco*, *Splinter Cell: Blacklist*, *DOOM*, and *Watch_Dogs 2*. He joined the team at Hangar 13 as a lead AI engineer in 2016, where he continues pushing character AI forward.

James Ryan is a PhD student of computer science at the University of California, Santa Cruz, California, working with the Expressive Intelligence Studio. He earned his BA in linguistics and MS in health informatics (with a minor in cognitive science) at the University of Minnesota, Minneapolis, Minnesota. His current research agenda spans two main topics: building autonomous agents who construct personal narratives out of their subjective experience in simulated worlds, and developing new technologies for freeform conversational interaction in games (by integrating systems for dialog management, natural language generation, and natural language understanding).

Jeet Shroff comes from a background in AI, animation, and gameplay programming and direction, where he has worked as a programmer and realization director on game titles across multiple genres and studios for the last 10 years. His industry experience includes working at Avalanche Studios, Ubisoft (Montreal), and Electronic Arts, where he has worked on successfully shipped titles for major franchises such as *FIFA* and *Far Cry 3*. Currently, he is a lead character programmer at Avalanche Studios, where he is responsible for the development of AI, animation, and player mechanics for an unannounced open-world AAA title. Jeet holds a bachelor of mathematics in computer science from the University of Waterloo, Ontario, Canada, and has spoken on open-world AI behavior and design at the Game Developers Conference.

Hendrik Skubch joined Square Enix in Japan in 2013 as an AI researcher, where he develops generic AI technologies for all aspects of game AI. In 2014, he joined a focused effort on *FINAL FANTASY XV* as a senior AI engineer. Before entering the game industry, he researched cooperative robotics and led a robotic soccer team within the RoboCup initiative. He received his PhD for work on robotic teams in 2012 from the University of Kassel, Kassel, Germany.

Cody Watts is a programmer and professional game developer. Since 2010, he has been working at BioWare Edmonton, where he is variously described by his coworkers as "a freaking genius" and "a space wizard ninja." While at BioWare, Cody has contributed to such AAA titles as *Dragon Age: Origins*, *Dragon Age II*, *Dragon Age: Inquisition* and *Mass Effect: Andromeda*. Cody holds a BSc and an MSc in computer science from the University of Calgary, Calgary, Canada, but more importantly, he beat *SpaceChem*—and that is *way* harder than defending a master's thesis. Follow Cody's latest adventures at www. codywatts.com.

Mieszko Zieliński has worked in the game industry throughout his professional life—that is close to 13 years at the time of writing—most of which focused on game AI. For the past eight years, he has been with Epic Games, with the past five spent on leading the AI system development in Unreal Engine 4. He has recently been micromanaging Paragon bots, which he found a very refreshing activity after the time spent on working for generic AI systems.

Robert Zubek is a game developer and cofounder at SomaSim, a Chicago-based indie studio founded in 2013 to create simulation games. Previously, he built large-scale online social games at Zynga, MMO game and analytics infrastructure at Three Rings Design, and console games at Electronic Arts/Maxis. Before joining the industry, he specialized in artificial intelligence and robotics research. Robert holds a PhD in computer science from Northwestern University, Evanston, Illinois, where he also received his previous computer science degrees.

Introduction

Steve Rabin's *Game AI Pro 360: Guide to Character Behavior* gathers all the cutting-edge information from his previous three Game AI Pro volumes into a convenient single source anthology that covers character behavior in game AI.

This volume is complete with articles by leading game AI programmers that focus on individual AI behavior such as character interactions, modelling knowledge, efficient simulation, difficulty balancing, and making decisions with case studies from both commercial and indie games.

This book, as well as each volume in the *Game AI Pro* series, is a testament to the generous community of game AI developers as well as the larger game development community. Everyone involved in this effort believes that sharing information is the single best way to rapidly innovate, grow and develop. Right now, the game AI community is larger than ever and we invite you to discover all the wonderful resources that are available.

In addition to reading about new game AI techniques in the *Game AI Pro* series, there are annual conferences, which are academic and developer-centric, all over the globe. Organized by developers, there is the Game AI summit at GDC in San Francisco each year and the game/AI conference in Europe. Organized by academia, there is the AAAI conference on Artificial Intelligence and Interactive Digital Entertainment (AIIDE) and the IEEE Conference on Computational Intelligence and Games. Outside of events, there are two communities that have also sprung up to help developers. The game AI Programmers Guild is a free professional group with more than 500 worldwide members (www.gameai.com) and there is a wonderful community of hobbyists and professionals at www.AIgameDev.com. We warmly welcome you to come and hang out with us at any one of these conferences or participate in one of the online communities.

Web Materials

Example programs and source code to accompany some of the chapters are available at http://www.gameaipro.com.

General System Requirements

The following is required to compile and execute the example programs:

- The DirectX August 2009 SDK
- DirectX 9.0 compatible or newer graphics card
- Windows 7 or newer
- Visual C++ .NET 2008 or newer

Updates of the example programs and source code will be updated as needed.

1

Infected AI in *The Last of Us*

Mark Botta

1.1 Introduction

In *The Last of Us* a fungal infection has devastated human beings. The pandemic corrupts the mind and has left most of the population grotesquely disfigured and relentlessly aggressive. The survivors have been forced to struggle not only against those overcome by the fungus (known as the Infected) but also against predatory groups of survivors (known as Hunters). This chapter will focus on the AI behind the Infected. Subsequent chapters will discuss the AI for Hunters and buddy characters.

It was our goal to make the Infected feel fundamentally different than Hunters, despite the fact that they use the same AI system. This was done with a modular AI architecture that allows us to easily add, remove, or change decision-making logic. This allows us to create characters that interact with the world in highly varied ways while keeping the code as simple as possible. Simple code is more maintainable, which is crucial when rapidly iterating on new ideas. Developing the Infected required continuous experimentation to discover what worked best. The more quickly new ideas were implemented, the sooner the designers were able to provide feedback. Keeping that cycle of refinement short enabled us to make the Infected feel grounded, entertaining, and believable.

The best way to achieve these goals is to make our characters not stupid before making them smart. Characters give the illusion of intelligence when they are placed in well-thought-out setups, are responsive to the player, play convincing animations and sounds, and behave in interesting ways. Yet all of this is easily undermined when they mindlessly

1

run into walls or do any of the endless variety of things that plague AI characters. Not only does eliminating these glitches provide a more polished experience, but it is amazing how much intelligence is attributed to characters that simply don't do stupid things.

1.2 The Infected

The Infected are humans who have succumbed to the parasitic *Cordyceps* fungus [Stark 13]. The infection ravages the body, leaving no trace of personality, compassion, or even self-preservation. The Infected are driven only by the instincts of the fungus.

Most survivors exist in prisonlike quarantine zones under martial law, but some choose to live outside of the quarantine zones, where they are free but constantly at risk of encountering the Infected or predatory gangs of Hunters.

We wanted the Infected to feel fundamentally different than the Hunters. Hunters work in groups, communicate with words and gestures, and protect each other. The player can see that their cold-blooded brutality is a means to survive. In contrast, the Infected seem chaotic and alien.

Table 1.1 summarizes the four types of Infected that represent the progression of the infection. Runners are the most common type. They are fast and often attack in uncoordinated groups. They can see and, like all Infected, their hearing is far more sensitive than that of the Hunters, making them just as effective in a dark room as they are on a sunlit street. Stalkers are similar to Runners but hide in dark areas and ambush prey. Clickers are visibly disfigured by the infection, with masses of fungus distorting their features and leaving them blind. They have developed a type of echolocation to compensate. They are slower than Runners but have a deadly frenzy attack and ignore melee attacks that don't use weapons. Bloaters are highly disfigured, blind, slow, and heavily armored. They grab and kill any character within reach, making melee attacks ineffective. They throw growths from their bodies that burst into disorienting clouds of irritating dust.

1.2.1 Senses

Our characters rely on their senses to reveal enemies and distractions in their environment. They track how and when they sense each entity and focus on the one that is the most threatening. All Infected, even Runners and Stalkers, rely primarily on hearing.

The sensory system does not reason about the actual audio heard in the game. Instead, logical sound events are generated specifically for this purpose. This gave the game designers more control, allowing them to specify which sounds are heard at what range

Table 1.1 Characteristics of Infected Character Types

Type	Runner	Stalker	Clicker	Bloater
Speed	Fast	Fast	Medium	Slow
Vision	Limited	Limited	Blind	Blind
Rarity	Common	Uncommon	Uncommon	Rare
Combat	Attack in groups	Ambush in dark areas	Melee frenzy, limited melee vulnerability	Armored, ranged attack, invulnerable to melee

by which character type. It also allowed sound designers to add or modify the game's audio without impacting the AI.

Wherever possible, we tried to correlate the logical sound events with actual audio, so that the player would be able to understand (and predict) the reactions of the Infected. There were exceptions, however. In particular, we wanted the AI to be able to sense nearby stationary targets, so we created a logical *breathing* sound that propagates over a very short range but has no audio.

Logical sounds are broadcast over a radius set by the designer, and any character within that radius—whether Infected or not—can hear it. Of course, not all characters hear equally well. We wanted the Infected to hear roughly six times better than the Hunters. We also wanted to be able to vary their hearing sensitivity based on their current behavior. For example, the Infected do not hear as well when they are unaware of the player. This makes it easier for the player to be stealthy, which slows the pace of the encounter, giving the player more opportunity to observe and plan. Thus, for a particular character type in a particular behavior, the radius of a logical sound is multiplied by a tunable value to give the effective radius within which that character will hear the sound.

Similar to actual audio, logical sounds are partially occluded by walls and obstacles. This was done to prevent the characters from hearing through walls as well as to reinforce the player's natural tendency to keep obstacles between them and the Infected. Each time a logic sound event is broadcast, rays are cast from each character within the sound radius to the source of the sound to determine the level of occlusion. The logical sound is broadcast to all characters in range that are not completely occluded.

In order to further differentiate the Infected from the Hunters, we wanted them to be more difficult to approach stealthily. It is a common video game trope to communicate stealthy movement to the player via crouch animations: when crouching, the player can approach another character from behind without being discovered. In *The Last of Us*, this was true of Hunters, but approaching the Infected with impunity while crouched made them feel considerably less dangerous. Our solution was to scale the broadcast radius of logical movement sounds with the speed of the player. This allows approaching the Infected more quickly from farther away but requires moving more slowly at melee range. To communicate this to the player, the Infected enter an agitated state when they start to hear noise, which gives the player a chance to respond before being discovered.

This raises an important point. Communicating the intent of the characters to the player is vital. We rejected some game features simply because they could not be communicated well. For example, Clickers make a barking sound that is an ornamental remnant of a more ambitious design. We originally wanted them to use a type of echolocation to build a local model of the environment (similar to how bats hunt and navigate). Each time that they barked, we would update their mental model of the local area by turning their vision on momentarily. This gave the character a sensory snapshot of threats in the world, but it did not communicate well and confused players that were *seen* by a blind character. We considered giving the bark a visual effect like a ripple of distortion washing over the environment but ultimately decided that this seemed too unrealistic. In the end, we abandoned this approach because it was complex and difficult to convey to the player.

1.2.2 Distractions

When Hunters see the beam of a flashlight or are hit by a brick, they can infer that some-body is nearby. The Infected lack this insight and react only to the stimulus itself. For example, they are drawn to the sound of a thrown object landing rather than deducing the existence of the character that threw it. This response empowered the player to manipulate the Infected and made bricks and bottles as valuable as any weapon.

This response was consistent with their instinctive behavior but it trivialized some encounters. This was particularly problematic when the player used a Molotov cocktail. The sound of the breaking bottle would attract all nearby Infected who would follow each other into the flames, become engulfed, and die. This was entertaining, but much too easy. We solved this by limiting the number of characters that could be affected by the flames. Molotov cocktails are expensive to craft and should be very effective, but not so effective that they take the challenge out of the game.

The Last of Us also allows players to create smoke bombs, which are used to break line of sight and mask the movement of the player. In principle, these should be ineffective against the Infected because they rely so heavily on their hearing, but again, that would take the fun out of the game. Instead, we had them occlude hearing as well as vision. Thus, after being attracted by the detonation of a smoke bomb, the Infected enter the cloud and become essentially blind and deaf. The player is rewarded with the opportunity to flee or to move among the distracted Infected strangling Runners and dispatching Clickers with shivs.

1.3 AI System

Our AI system makes a distinction between the high-level decision logic (*skills*) that decides what the character should do and the low-level capabilities (*behaviors*) that implement those decisions. This separation allows characters with different high-level skills to reuse the same low-level behaviors. For example, movement is encapsulated in the *move-to* behavior that is invoked by many different skills. Furthermore, in this behavior, the decision of where to go is independent of how the character decides to get there. One character may use the *move-to* behavior to move stealthily in the shadows, while another charges forward.

Skills decide what to do based on the motivations and capabilities of the character, as well as the current state of the environment. They answer questions like *Do I want to attack, hide, or flee?* and *What is the best place for me to be?* Once a decision is made, behaviors are invoked to implement it. For example, if movement is required, the skill may invoke the *move-to* behavior and then wait for it to succeed or fail.

The *move-to* behavior attempts to reach the destination using whatever capabilities are available to it. It answers questions like *Which route should I take?* and *Which animations should I play?* It generates paths, avoids obstacles, selects animations to traverse the environment, and ultimately reports the results to the parent skill.

1.3.1 Philosophy

As a general rule, characters don't need complex high-level decision-making logic in order to be believable and compelling and to give the illusion of intelligence. What they need is to appear grounded by reacting to and interacting with the world around them in believable ways. Of course, they also need to avoid doing stupid things. Characters in *The Last of Us* can see and hear threats and distractions, they can navigate by climbing over obstacles and jumping gaps, they can look around corners, they can respond to fire, and they can search for prey. By building a rich set of behaviors that allow characters to interact with the world and picking appropriate behaviors even in fairly simple ways, we create characters that draw the player into the drama of the moment, which sell the story and make the experience meaningful.

In order to be able to reuse skills as widely as possible, we needed to keep them flexible but well encapsulated and decoupled, so that each skill could be adjusted to fit its particular use without affecting other skills. This was very valuable in the late stages of development. Features changed quickly, and it was important to be able to insulate the rest of the code from unstable prototypes. Our modular approach also made it easy to completely remove any failed experiments without fear of leaving any remnants behind. This allowed us to experiment with major changes to the AI right up to the end of the project. For example, Stalkers were conceived of and implemented only a few months before the game shipped.

1.3.2 Data-Driven Design

One key to keeping the code general was to never refer to any of the character types in code, but instead to specify sets of characteristics that define each type of character. All of the Infected character types share a single C++ class and are differentiated only by the set of skills and the values of the tuning variables in their data files. For example, the code refers to the *vision type* of the character instead of testing if the character is a Runner or a Clicker. This may sound like a minor distinction, but it is central to our efforts to keep the code general. Rather than spreading the character definitions as conditional checks throughout the code, it centralizes them in tunable data. This gives designers control over character variations, rather than requiring them to request changes from the AI team, which would slow their iteration times considerably. Furthermore, when adding a new type of Infected or changing an existing type in a fundamental way, there is no need to hunt down all of the places in the code that refer to the character. There aren't any! Just add or remove skills, behaviors, and tuning variables, and everything is kept modular and flexible.

This approach requires constant vigilance. There were many occasions when we were tempted to add a check for a specific character type for *just one thing*. Unfortunately, that *one thing* tends to proliferate as code is extended and reused, or as features are added, or just for convenience when testing. The lesson here is to stay true to your design principles because that consistency will pay off in terms of stability and ease of implementing new features.

An additional benefit became clear when we added the difficulty levels to the game. Because of memory and performance restrictions, difficulty couldn't be tuned by adding more characters to encounters. Keeping all of the character-specific data tunable made it straightforward to configure the difficulty settings for each character type individually. For each character type, designers modified the thresholds at which the Infected would respond to stimuli. For example, at lower difficulty settings, Clickers respond to nearby stimuli by turning and barking, whereas at higher difficulty settings, they are less forgiving and will often chase the player at the slightest provocation.

1.3.3 Implementation

The AI for a specific type of character is implemented as a set of skills that invoke a hierarchy of behaviors. Both skills and behaviors are implemented as straightforward finite-state machines. Skills tend to be tailored to specific character types, while behaviors are more widely reused. For example, Hunters and Infected characters do not share any skills but they share most of their behaviors.

Each type of character maintains a prioritized list of skills. These are tested one at a time from highest to lowest priority to determine if they are valid to run. Testing stops when a valid skill is found. The last skill in the list must always be valid or the character could get into an uncontrolled state and become unresponsive, freeze, walk into a wall, or otherwise look stupid. Skills run until they are completed or are interrupted by a higher priority skill.

1.3.4 Debugging

Maintaining the separation between skills and behaviors has another benefit. We can debug a character by replacing the skills with logic that drives the high-level decisions from a game controller. Of course, nonplayer characters take input differently than a player character. For example, they move to specific locations as opposed to taking directional input from a thumb stick. Conversely, they have controls that the player character doesn't have. They can select from several demeanors (e.g., whether to appear aggressive or relaxed), they have numerous gestures for communication, they have to select look and aim points, and they have a rich set of behaviors to choose from. There are far more inputs available to nonplayer characters than there are buttons on a controller!

To support all of these inputs, an on-screen menu appears when a character is selected for debugging. From here, we can put the character into the desired state, select the desired behavior, and use a cursor to select a destination. We also have convenience options to teleport the character and repeat the last move command, making it much easier to refine animations and behaviors without needing to rely on waiting for the skills to use them.

1.4 Skills and Behaviors

Table 1.2 contains the skills used by each type of Infected, sorted by priority. Priorities specify which skills should be allowed to interrupt each other. For example, the *chase* skill is allowed to interrupt the *search* skill but can be interrupted by the *on-fire* skill. The *wander*

Table 1.2 Prioritized Skills for Infected Character Types

Runner	Stalker	Clicker	Bloater
On-fire	On-fire	On-fire	On-fire
Chase	Ambush	Chase	Throw
Search	Sleep	Search	Chase
Follow	Wander	Follow	Search
Sleep		Sleep	Follow
Wander		Wander	Sleep
			Wander

skill is the fallback for all types of Infected and is always valid. Conceptually, if the Infected aren't busy doing anything else, they'll be wandering around their environment.

Our goal was to share as much of the AI between the Infected characters as possible so that new character types could be added easily. When development started, it was unknown how many character variations there would be or how they would behave. We experimented with different types of game play and a variety of character types. Each variation went through several iterations before it showed promise and was kept for further refinement or until the potential was exhausted and it was cut. As a result, most of the skills are shared by all Infected character types. Only two skills are used by a single character type: the *ambush* skill used by the Stalker and the *throw* skill used by the Bloater. The Infected spend most of their time in the *wander* and *chase* skills. Similarly, most of these skills invoke behaviors that are also used by the Hunters. There are only two behaviors that are unique to the Infected: the *infected-canvass* behavior and the *infected-listen* behavior.

1.4.1 *Search* Skill

Hunters have a complex search skill that enables them to uncover all hidden locations in an encounter in a coordinated way. The Infected, on the other hand, are not particularly well organized or thorough, so an Infected-specific search skill was needed. The *search* skill becomes valid to run when an Infected loses track of the player during a chase. The search is not exhaustive; they eventually lose interest and resume wandering around. The intent of the skill is to keep the player moving as the character explores nearby hiding places.

Hiding places are polygons on the navigation mesh that are not visible from other parts of the navigation mesh. When the search begins, a graph of *search points* is generated that reveal hiding places. A search point is added at the center of the polygon containing the last known location of the target entity. A breadth-first traversal visits neighboring polygons until line of sight to the search point is broken. A new search point is added at the center of the parent polygon (i.e., the last polygon with line of sight to the previous search point). This process continues until the entire search area is visited or a fixed number of search points have been added. The result is a graph of points with visibility to each other and to all of the hiding places around them.

Points are selected on the search graph based on the predicted location of the player [Straatman 06]. This has the effect of propagating desirable search points over time, which the Infected explore in a natural-looking search pattern, and puts pressure on players who tend to stay put. When an Infected reaches a search point, it briefly investigates before moving on.

When investigating, we wanted the Infected to appear to move around frantically and cover as much of the immediate area as possible without looking planned or methodical. Also, since search points can be generated anywhere on the navigation mesh, the area to search could be an arbitrary shape and size and may contain obstacles like debris or furniture. The *infected-canvass* behavior was designed to meet these requirements. It works as follows (and is illustrated in Figure 1.1):

1. A logical grid is placed over the area covered by the *canvass radius* and centered on the Infected.
2. Obstacles and the area outside of the canvass radius are marked as *seen*, leaving an area of cells that need to be checked.

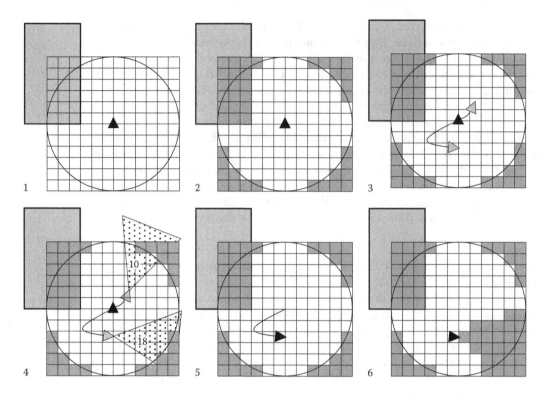

Figure 1.1

Selecting an animation in the *infected-canvass* behavior near an obstacle.

3. The invoking skill provides the behavior with a collection of animations that it can use. We determine the location and orientation that the character will have at the end of each of these animations.

4. The number of *unseen* cells in a sensory wedge in front of the character is counted for each animation. The wedge need not match the area covered by the actual senses. A larger wedge gives more coverage for a faster search and a smaller wedge gives a more thorough search.

5. Animations that result in more *unseen* cells are more desirable. Animations that were played recently are less desirable. The most desirable animation is played, moving the character.

6. When the animation has completed, the cells in the sensory wedge are marked *seen* and the process repeats at the new location from step 3.

The *Infected-canvass* behavior never explicitly selects the direction the character moves—it is based solely on the available animations. This made the code much simpler and animators were not restricted to producing animations in a fixed number of directions, which gave them the freedom to create a larger variety of expressive performances. Designers had control over the canvass radius and how long the character continues to canvass. For variety, the behavior includes sets of animations that move the character both near

1. Infected AI in *The Last of Us*

and far. In a small area, the character uses the near set of animations and turns quickly to look in all directions in an unpredictable (and seemingly random) order. In larger areas, the far set of animations are added to the mix, resulting in the character moving across the canvass area in short and long bursts. The process is not exhaustive, but it is convincingly frantic, it looks organic, and it is very flexible. The behavior was used by several other Infected skills in addition to the *search* skill.

1.4.2 *Chase* Skill

Most of the Infected have almost trivially simple combat tactics: when an entity is sensed, they get to it as fast as possible and attack it. This is done by the *chase* skill.

When an entity is first encountered, the Infected turns toward the stimulus and screams to alert the player that they have been discovered. The *chase* skill does this by invoking the *surprise* behavior that selects from a set of animations that orient the character in the appropriate direction.

Next, the *chase* skill invokes the *move-to* behavior, which provides an interface to the navigation system and is responsible for moving the character to a location or entity. As the entity moves through the environment, the *move-to* behavior continuously updates the path, leaving the parent skill to simply monitor for success or failure. This is one of the key advantages of the modular behavior system—it allows us to keep the high-level logic in the skills very simple.

During the chase, the character will occasionally pause to reorient, giving the player more opportunity to hide or prepare an attack. Instead of simply pausing movement, the *infected-canvass* behavior is used for a very short duration in a small area and with a special set of animations, which gives the Infected the appearance of frantically trying to reacquire the player during the chase.

1.4.3 *Follow* Skill

Unlike Hunters, the Infected do not communicate with one another. They share no information anywhere in the code. This is consistent with the idea that they are not intelligent and only respond instinctively to the stimuli in their environment. Consequently, if an Infected senses the player and starts to chase, any nearby Infected that do not directly sense the player are oblivious. Although this makes sense, in practice it made the Infected seem a bit too insensitive to their environment.

As an alternative, we added the *follow* skill, which allows one character to follow another that is chasing something. The following character does not receive any information about the entity being chased; it just has the compulsion to follow along. Conceptually, the Infected seek the opportunity to claim the unknown prey for themselves. As a result, when an Infected is alerted and starts chasing the player, it may pick up others along the way, but as the player expects, the alerted character will be the first to arrive.

1.4.4 *Ambush* Skill

The *ambush* skill is a combat skill used by Stalkers that replaces the *chase* skill used by all of the other Infected types. It was created late in the development of the game while experimenting with different character types. The character types we had were solid but we wanted more variety. We experimented with a light-sensitive character that the player could hold at bay with a flashlight. This showed promise but when the characters reacted quickly, they didn't feel dangerous, and when they reacted more slowly, the flashlight didn't feel effective. After a few iterations, we decided to take advantage of the dark in a different way. The idea was to have the character move from cover to cover, providing only glimpses to the player in dark environments. They would lay in wait until the player wandered too close, then attack and run back into cover. This simple concept proved very effective at heightening the sense of horror. In encounters with Stalkers, the player naturally became more defensive and approached each corner with caution. Keeping the Infected out of sight also served to hide the number of characters in the encounter, which made tracking down the last Stalker as tense as the first.

Ambush is the only Infected-specific skill that uses cover. Cover locations are selected using a system that evaluates points in the environment based on how suitable they are to ambush the player or to retreat after an attack. This system is shared with the Hunters and will be described in more detail in the chapter describing their AI.

1.4.5 *Throw* Skill

The Bloater is the only Infected character with a projectile attack. The fungus has swollen its body into a misshapen mass of armored plates and bulbous fungal growths. The Bloater rips these growths from various armored plates and throws them ahead of the moving player to produce a cloud of particles that briefly slow movement. The armor plates spawning these growths can be destroyed, and the *throw* skill plays animations that select from other plates until they are all destroyed and the Bloater dies. Until then, there is no limit to the number of growths a Bloater can throw, which prevents it from becoming less challenging as the encounter progresses.

1.4.6 *On-Fire* Skill

It may be odd to consider reacting to being engulfed in flame as an AI skill because, unlike other skills, it doesn't show intent and isn't a conscious decision. However, the goal here is not so much to show the intent of the character as it is to allow it to react to its situation and to make it more believable and entertaining.

The *on-fire* skill works by invoking the *infected-canvass* behavior briefly in a small area, with a custom set of animations. This causes the character to flail and dart around chaotically in an arbitrary environment without running into walls. It also provides emergent variation in the reaction because it combines several smaller reactions for the full effect. This is a great example of a case where we were able to reuse the same behavior with different contents (in this case, different animations) in order to achieve a very different, customized, and compelling result.

1.4.7 *Wander* Skill

The *wander* skill is the lowest priority skill for all of the Infected character types. It is the fallback that is used when nothing else is valid to run. When the Infected are not agitated, they will move throughout the environment either randomly or in predictable patterns. The challenge was to do this in such a way that the player is forced to make tactical decisions about when to move, distract, or attack.

Designers can specify whether the character wanders on a fixed route or randomly. Fixed routes require laying out a spline in the level editor and specifying environmental interactions at various points. These can be as simple as pausing and looking around or as complex as triggering a brief behavior (such as scavenging through debris) before returning to moving along the spline. Random wandering selects a random polygon on the navigation mesh as a destination. As the character moves, it keeps track of the polygons it visits. On arrival, it randomly selects a polygon that hasn't been visited and continues to wander. This has the effect of covering a large area in an unpredictable way.

Both types of wandering have their uses. A fixed route is predictable, which makes it useful for crafting stealth encounters where the player is encouraged to deduce the pattern and avoid it. Random movement is useful for covering a large area in unpredictable ways, offering the player a different challenge. In practice, fixed routes are used for the initial setup of an encounter, and random movement is used after leaving combat when the character may be far away from the original route.

1.4.8 *Sleep* Skill

Designers can configure the Infected to sleep when idle instead of using the *wander* skill. This is an idle state that greatly reduces the sensitivity of the senses, giving the player the opportunity to avoid, distract, or dispatch the character more easily. This skill was also useful for creating sentries at choke points throughout the game, since sleeping Infected stay where they are placed.

Sleeping characters react to disturbances in several ways. If the player moves too quickly or too near a sleeping Infected, it will stir briefly before settling back into slumber. This is feedback to inform the player that they should exercise more caution. If the player makes a loud noise from a great enough distance, the Infected will wake up and use the *infected-canvass* behavior to move about a small area searching for the disturbance before going back to sleep. If the player continues to disturb the character or is sufficiently loud, it will wake enraged and *chase* the disturbance. When the chase ends the Infected will wander through the environment instead of going back to sleep.

1.5 Conclusion

The Infected are a compelling part of a complex world. They are the result of design, art, sound, animation, and programming coming together to make characters that fit seamlessly into the environment, making the world more believable. They are entertaining characters and are worthy opponents that command respect but can be overcome with skill.

The capabilities provided by the behaviors allow the skills to focus on high-level decisions. This simplified the development process and enabled new ideas to be rapidly explored in order to refine the Infected into engaging opponents. Keeping the code simple and modular made it more maintainable and stable. This made it easier to isolate glitches that made the characters look stupid. Eliminating these problems went a long way toward making the Infected look smart.

Skills and behaviors are a small part of a complex AI character, but they provide the decision making needed to make the character respond convincingly to the player. Keeping it simple was the key. Using tuning values that were independent of the type of character allowed all of the Infected to share the same skills and behaviors but respond in ways that were unique and interesting.

References

[Stark 13] Stark, C. 2013. The creepy, real science behind "The Last of Us." http://mashable.com/2013/07/26/the-last-of-us/ (accessed September 10, 2014).

[Straatman 06] Straatman, R., A. Beij, and W. van der Sterren. 2006. Dynamic tactical position evaluation. In *AI Programming Wisdom 3*, ed. S. Rabin, pp. 389–403. Boston, MA: Charles River Media.

2

Human Enemy AI in *The Last of Us*

Travis McIntosh

2.1 Introduction

In the previous chapter, we discussed the overall design philosophy and the AI techniques behind the Infected. In this chapter, we will discuss a question that relates to the human opponents in *The Last of Us*. When we started prototyping the human enemy AI, we began with this question: *How do we make the player believe that their enemies are real enough that they feel bad about killing them?* Answering that one question drove the entire design of the enemy AI.

Answering that question required more than just hiring the best voice actors, the best modelers, and the best animators, although it *did* require all of those things. It also required solving an AI problem. Because if we couldn't make the player believe that these roving bands of survivors were thinking and acting together like real people, then no amount of perfectly presented mocap was going to prevent the player from being pulled out of the game whenever an NPC took cover on the wrong side of a doorway or walked in front of his friend's line of fire.

To begin with, our enemies had to be dangerous. If they acted like cannon fodder, the player would treat them like cannon fodder, so the player had to feel like each and every human they encountered was a threat. They also needed to coordinate, or at least to appear to coordinate. A roving band of survivors needs to work together to survive, just as Joel and Ellie must work together, and without some sort of coordination, they would appear subhuman. They also needed to care about their own safety. These were not suicide bombers. They were survivors. They should be as careful with their own lives as the player would be with theirs.

They needed to make good choices about where to go and when to go there, and more than that, they needed to be intelligent about *how* to get there. When they lost the player, they needed to communicate that fact to each other in a way that would be obvious to the player, and when their friends died, they needed to notice.

The design of *The Last of Us* also called for completely dynamic gameplay. Rarely were we guaranteed the location of the player when combat began, and at any point, the player could force the NPCs into a brand new setup from a different location. This meant that little of the NPC behavior could be scripted by hand. Instead, the NPCs had to be able to understand and analyze the play space, then adapt to the actions of the player.

Putting these concepts together with a number of visual and audio bells and whistles produced human enemies that could be enjoyable to play and just believable enough that, sometimes, every now and again, the player cared about who they were killing.

2.2 Building Blocks

Every AI system builds upon several key low-level systems. *The Last of Us* uses triangulated navmeshes, which are a fairly straightforward approach to navigation. The navmeshes are fairly coarse, and so we have a second-pass system that uses a 2D grid centered around every character on which are rasterized all static and dynamic blockers. This allows for short but very good paths, while the high-level system allows us to plan our overall route between distant points.

Pathfinding on navigation meshes is fast, especially utilizing the PS3's SPUs. We did between 20 and 40 pathfinds every frame utilizing approximately 4 ms of SPU time. Pathfinding through navigation maps (a fixed sized grid that surrounded each NPC for detailed path analysis), by contrast, was expensive enough that we limited the game to one per frame, with each NPC needing to wait for their turn.

One system that was new to *The Last of Us* was the *exposure map*. Early in the project, we found that in order for the AI to make good decisions about which path to take, we needed information about what the player could see and what he couldn't see. Exposure maps were our representation of this information.

We initially implemented visibility checks by casting rays toward the player from a number of different points on the NPC's current path and then using that information to decide whether the path was a good one or not. Unfortunately, this didn't work very well. Not only was it slow, but it didn't allow us to choose different paths based on the visibility information, which is what we really wanted. We then came up with concept of an exposure map, as shown in Figure 2.1. An exposure map is simply a 2D bitmap overlaid on the navigation mesh. In the exposure map, a one indicates visibility and a zero indicates occlusion.

In order to make calculating the exposure map fast, we embedded a simple height map inside of every navigation mesh. The height map used an 8-bit integer to represent the height of the world at every point on every navigation mesh. On the SPUs, we could then do very simple raycast out from the origin point in a 360° circle. Because we were working only in integer space and on the SPUs, we could parallelize this fairly easily. We then allowed the job to take multiple frames to complete. The end result is that we could continually calculate

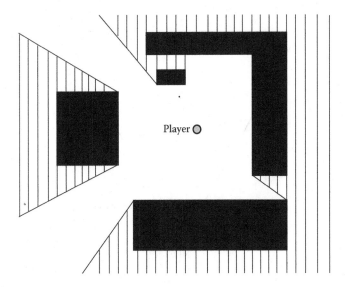

Figure 2.1

The exposure map covers everything an entity can see.

an exposure map for what the player could see, as well as an exposure map that showed everything any NPC could see as a simple bitmap using around 2–3 ms of SPU time.

Because the exposure map was, in fact, a bitmap, we often used it as a cost in our navigation function. The cost of traveling from one node to another was increased by integrating across this bitmap and multiplying by a scale factor. So, for example, we could use our standard pathfinding algorithm to find the best route from an NPC to the player, or we could add the exposure map as an additional cost and the path would minimize the NPC's exposure to the player's line of sight. Our first implementation of flanking was done using this exact algorithm, and it produced surprisingly good results in the static case.

2.3 AI Perception

One of the fundaments of AI in any game, especially a game focused on stealth, is AI perception. In the *Uncharted* series, AI used a few simple systems to determine their awareness of the world.

First, their sight we determined by a simple frustum and raycasts to check for occlusion. At the start of *The Last of Us*, we used this same system, as shown in Figure 2.2.

Problems arose in playtesting, however. Often, players right next to the NPC would be unseen, while NPCs too far away were noticed, simply because the cone we used for testing was not adequate to represent real vision. The fundamental issue was that, when close, we needed a larger angle of view, but at a distance we needed a smaller one. Using a simple rule—the angle of view for an NPC is inversely proportional to distance—we reinvented our view frustum to be much more effective, as shown in Figure 2.3.

Just because the player could be seen on one frame did not mean the NPCs had instant awareness of him. When an NPC saw the player, he would start a timer. Each frame the

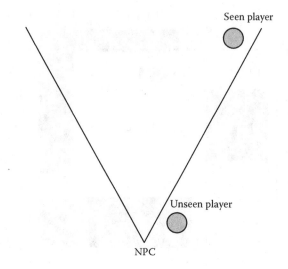

Figure 2.2

The simplest form of perception testing for NPCs had issues.

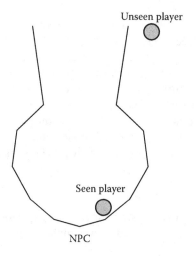

Figure 2.3

This more complex form of vision cone produced better results.

player was seen, the timer was incremented. Each frame the player was unseen, the timer was decremented. The player did not count as perceived until the timer reached a specified value (around 1 or 2 seconds for the typical NPC). When in combat, this threshold was much lower, and when the NPC had yet to perceive the player in its lifetime (i.e., the player is in stealth), this threshold was much higher.

We tried a number of different approaches to casting rays to check for occlusion. Our initial implementation involved rays to nearly every joint on Joel's body. Each joint was weighted, and the weighted average was compared against a threshold (typically 60%). If the sum was higher, then the player is counted as visible.

This produced mixed results. Although it was a decent approximation of when Joel was visible and eliminated the edge cases of being seen when just your head or finger was visible, players found it difficult to anticipate whether a given cover point was safe or not, because of the complexity of the casts.

After some experimentation, we found that we could use a single point on Joel's body instead. The location of that point would vary depending on whether we were in combat or stealth, as shown in Figure 2.4. If the player was in stealth, then the point is located in the center of the player's chest. If the player has engaged an NPC in combat, the point moved to the top of the player's head. This allows for player favoring perception in stealth while maintaining good visibility in combat.

Of note, the NPCs did not cheat with regard to knowing the player's location in most circumstances. When the player was perceived, the NPC would create an entity object with location and time stamp and then signal all other NPCs with the player's new location. If the player was not perceived by any NPCs, his location was never updated, instead remained in the previous location.

The combat cycle of *The Last of Us* was then as follows: The player showed himself, either visibly or by shooting his gun. The NPCs would surround him as best as they could and then began to advance on his position. If they had advanced as close as they could and they hadn't seen the player in a long enough period (10 s or more), a single NPC was chosen to approach the player's position to see if he was still there. If he was not, the NPCs then transitioned into the search behavior.

In our original focus tests, this combat cycle took far too long—nearly 2 min on average. Quite often, the player would have moved on long ago and would feel like the NPCs were not responsive. Our solution to this problem was to cheat. If the player moved further than 5 m from where the NPCs thought he was, he was considered to have snuck away, and we forced an NPC to approach his position immediately, so that they could enter search more quickly. This reduced the combat cycle to about 30 s and worked very well for pacing purposes.

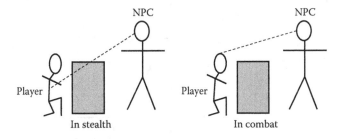

Figure 2.4

The left image shows that in stealth, the raycast point is placed on the player's chest, in order to favor the player. The right image shows that once combat has been initiated, the raycast point is placed much higher onto the top of the head.

2.4 Cover and Posts

Where to stand/take cover is one of the most fundamental decisions AIs need to make, and it is also one of the hardest. In order to properly rate and evaluate the best cover and open locations, you first need to gather a set of potential locations. We called these *posts*.

We had two distinct types of posts. The firsts were cover posts. These were gathered for each NPC in a radius around the NPC's location. Candidates were any cover spot facing away from the threat (all possible cover spots were precalculated by a tool analyzing the collision mesh). After we gathered the closest 20 cover spots for each NPC, we submitted them as a single job. Each frame, we would cast up to 160 rays to these different spots, each cover spot requiring 4 rays to determine whether the NPC could shoot and hit their target. When all of the rays for a given set of cover were complete, those covers where every ray was blocked were rejected, as shown in Figure 2.5.

We called the second type of post as an open post. Open posts were points in the world around the player. Primarily, these were used to find a good location for the NPCs to check the player's last known location when they were sent forward to begin a search. We again cast rays from these locations to the last known player position and rejected any whose raycast failed. In addition, we did a pathfind, limited to 20 per frame, from every NPC to every viable post for use in our post selectors.

Once we had a valid set of posts, we could then do analysis to select the location the NPC should use. Since every NPC behavior is significantly different, this used different criteria depending on what the NPC was doing at the time. We called these *post selectors*. Post selectors were defined in our LISP-based scripting language, with an example shown in Listing 2.1. We had 17 different post selectors when we shipped *The Last of Us*.

Each post selector defined what type of post it was interested in (in this case, cover and a number of different criteria). The criteria were different for each different selector and could easily be iterated on at runtime by reloading the script.

Of particular interest is the criterion **ai-criterion-static-pathfind-not-near-player**. Many times, during focus tests, players would complain that NPCs would rush forward to take cover. With some debugging, we determined that the issue was that a particular cover

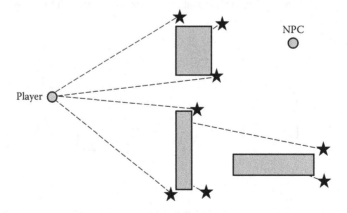

Figure 2.5

Any cover post whose raycast is blocked is rejected.

2. Human Enemy AI in *The Last of Us*

Listing 2.1. This script defines a post selector which locates a good place to hide.

```
(panic
  :post-type (ai-post-type cover)
  :criteria (ai-criteria
              (ai-criterion-path-valid)
              (ai-criterion-within-close-in-dist)
              (ai-criterion-available)
              (ai-criterion-static-pathfind-not-near-player)
              (ai-criterion-not-behind-the-player)
              (ai-criterion-distance
                :curve (new-ai-point-curve
                        ([distance 3.0] [value 0.0])
                        ([distance 5.0] [value 1.0])
                       )
              )
            )
  )
)
```

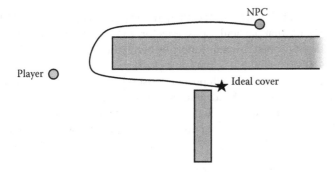

Figure 2.6

Sometimes the best cover could not be determined without a path. If the path to the cover required running toward the player for too long, as in this example, then the cover would be rejected.

was the best cover choice, but in order to pathfind there, the NPC would need to move toward the player, so that they could then move away again, as shown in Figure 2.6.

The solution was to write a criterion that used the pathfind information we had for every NPC to every viable cover. These paths were calculated in a round robin fashion and took about a 1/2 s to refresh, gathered at the same time as the cover-to-player raycasts. We would then analyze the path the NPC would take to each cover point, and if that path involved running toward the player for an extended period, then we would reject that cover.

There were, in fact, two major systems operating in parallel. The first system gathered pathfinding information, raycasts, etc. The second simply processed these data using the post selectors. Since the source data were all gathered on previous frames, these post selectors could be evaluated for very low cost on the SPUs. Each criterion would produce a float value normalized between zero and one; all of the criteria for a given post selector and a

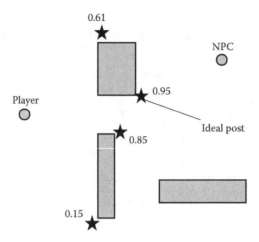

Figure 2.7

Every post is rated and the one with the highest number wins.

given post would then be multiplied together, and the resulting value would be that particular post's rating for that particular post selector. Next, all the posts would be sorted by rating, and the ideal post determined, simply by being the post with the highest rating, as shown in Figure 2.7.

Ratings would be different for each post per post selector and unique NPC. A post that was rejected for *panic* might be the ideal for *advance*. Note that all of the criteria for all of the posts and post selectors were evaluated continuously, so there was no delay when the NPC switched states—the ideal post for any given post selector was always available.

2.5 Skills, States, and Behaviors

The NPC's top-level states, which we called *skills*, were part of an FSM. Skills were prioritized, and each skill queried every frame whether it wished to run. The skill with the highest priority won. Examples of skills include *panic*, *advance*, *melee*, *gun combat*, *hide*, *investigate*, *scripted*, and *flank*.

Each skill included its own state machine. So, for example, *gun combat* could be in the *advance* or the *back away* state. Note that these were high-level states and didn't typically directly interface with the animation or pathfinding systems. Instead, a separate object known as a *behavior* would be pushed onto a behavior stack. Behaviors were on much lower level and were much simpler than the top-level states. Examples include MoveToLocation, StandAndShoot, and TakeCover.

2.6 Stealth

Stealth was handled by two separate skills. The *investigate* skill understood how to respond to a distraction sound and had a custom post selector. If the NPCs were in their standard scripted states—fully controlled by designer-created scripts that would tell them where to move, when to move, and even what audio dialog to play—then when an audio gameplay

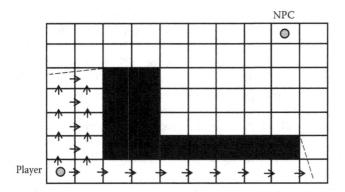

Figure 2.8

Search map locations spread out until within an NPC's line of sight.

event signaled a distraction, NPCs would request the role of an Investigator. Whichever NPC got that role would then walk to the ideal post as specific by the custom post selector and play an animation. If they found nothing, they would return to their previous location and pick up their script where it left off.

This was the case if the player had not been located yet. If the NPCs were already aware of the player, they entered the *search* state. *Search* involved procedurally partitioning the map and sending the NPCs to search it. Where to search was solved by the *search map*. The search map was a series of grid cells. If the player's location was known, all cells would be empty except the player's current location. Once the player's location was lost, however, the active cells would then bleed into their neighbors over time, and the potential location of the player would spread out to cover the map, as shown in Figure 2.8. Using the exposure map, any cells currently visible to an NPC would be cleared each frame. The result was a grid of cells that represented, roughly, the potential locations of the player from the NPC's perspective, who could then search in a relatively intelligent fashion.

2.7 Lethality

Games can create threatening enemies in a few ways. Enemies can take a lot of damage—in *The Last of Us* this broke immersion since you were supposed to be fighting humans. The number of enemies could be high—this directly contradicts our goal of making the player care about each and every kill. The enemies could deal a lot of damage—a possibility. The enemies could be very good at being hard to hit—another possibility.

We began by focusing on a concept we called *lethality*. Lethality meant that if a single enemy could kill the player, then every shot was frightening. One of the simplest and most successful things we did was make every shot the player received play a full body hit reaction. This meant that getting shot would not only deal significant damage but also take away control while the animation played out. In fact, it was the loss of control that most affected players. Those few moments of helplessness meant that every shot became a punctuation mark, a pause in the flow of the action that didn't let them forget their mistake.

Another way we made enemies lethal was by making sure to provide a threat whenever possible. This meant whenever an NPC had the ability to shoot the player, they would always choose to do that. With that said, it was only necessary for one NPC to be shooting the player at any given time; all other NPCs could spend their time taking cover, flanking, etc.

What this meant was that we needed a way for NPCs to coordinate with one another. We created a system we called the *Combat Coordinator*. The Combat Coordinator was simply a global object that managed each NPC's role. The roles include *Flanker*, *Approacher*, *Investigator*, *StayUpAndAimer*, and *OpportunisticShooter*.

Whenever a particular NPC desired a given role, they called the `RequestRole()` function on the Combat Coordinator. If that role was available, the function returned success, the NPC called `AcknowledgeRole()`, and no other NPC could take that role until they released it.

The purpose of the *OpportunisticShooter* role was to make sure there was at least one NPC focusing on shooting the player at any given time. If any NPC was able to see and shoot the player from their current location, they requested this role. Once they had the role, they instantly began shooting the player. This greatly increased the lethality of the NPCs. Note that when an NPC had this role, they would instantly stop whatever they were doing—even mid animation—and blend to standing and shooting at the player. In earlier playtests, they were noticeably slow in transitioning to shooting, with the result that oftentimes the player would be almost completely untouched when rushing.

2.8 Flanking

The role of the Combat Coordinator was not simply to be a gatekeeper to a few conceptual roles. In some cases, the coordinator would only allow a single, ideal NPC to take a given role. The best example of this is the *Flanker* role. Each NPC would run a pathfind in every frame to determine their best flank route. Each flank route would then be rated based on cost, and the coordinator would choose an ideal *Flanker* for the frame. If any NPC requested to flank the player but wasn't the ideal *Flanker*, their request would be rejected. Sometimes, as in the case of the *OpportunisticShooter*, we simply wished for the role to be taken as quickly as possible, so we would simply assign the role on a first come, first serve basis.

Although we originally used the exposure map to determine flanking, in practice this produced a number of issues. Because the exposure map changed as the player moved, often the flank routes could vary wildly from one frame to the next, and a corridor the algorithm identified as unexposed last frame could become exposed very quickly if the player was just around the corner.

The solution was to use a cost function based on the current *combat vector*. The combat vector was simply the current direction of combat from the player's perspective, calculated by averaging the NPC positions weighted by any shots that had been fired recently. Given the current combat vector, the cost function for flanking a given NPC was a fixed shape in the direction of that vector, as shown in Figure 2.9.

The closer to the center line (the line directly in the path of the combat vector), the higher the cost for pathfinding. The result of using this cost function was that flanking paths immediately attempted to move a large distance to the side and come around from behind, which was precisely what the player expected. In addition, the obstacles in the way were immaterial to how the cost function was created, and we instead let the pathfinding handle finding the path.

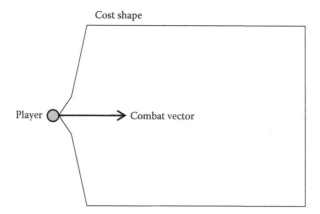

Figure 2.9

The combat shape rotates with the direction of the combat vector.

2.9 Polish

Once the AI decision making was in place, dialog could be layered in, animations could be polished, and setups could be scripted. Dialog in particular allowed the AI to communicate the decisions they make to the player, so that the NPCs could appear to be as intelligent as they sometimes were.

Then came focus testing, and more focus testing. Indeed, half of our implementation decisions were made in response to videos of players playing the game. In general, spatial analysis of the play space was perhaps the biggest win for us in terms of improving the AI's decision making. Combining that with the Combat Coordinator produced NPCs that made coordinated, informed decisions in a dynamic play space and appeared to be working together as a group.

2.10 Conclusion

In the end, we achieved our goal. The enemies had personality and had some sort of life, and most importantly, killing the enemies in *The Last of Us* was hard—not in the sense of difficulty but in a more emotional, more visceral sense. Because every enemy was a threat, every enemy felt more real and more alive, and because they felt alive, the player was able to build a small connection with them. The violence in *The Last of Us* was disturbing, not merely because of its graphic nature but because the player cared about the people they were attacking. The NPCs worked together, like real people. The NPCs fled and hid when threatened, like real people. The NPCs made good choices about where to go and how to get there, and most of the time they didn't destroy the illusion the player had immersed themselves in.

What we ended up with was not perfect by any means, but it answered the question of whether players cared about the people they were killing. They did.

3

Ellie: Buddy AI in *The Last of Us*

Max Dyckhoff

3.1 Introduction

In the last couple of chapters, you have read about the hunter and infected AI from Naughty Dog's third-person action adventure game *The Last of Us*. This chapter moves on to discuss the buddy AI.

The whole game focuses on relationships between characters and none more strongly than that of Ellie and Joel, the player's avatar. Ellie accompanies the player throughout most of the game, and we needed the player to love her companionship. We were acutely aware of the common pitfalls with AI companions: the risk of them turning into a tedious "escort" quest, generally getting underfoot, or turning into mindless drones with no agency in the world. We had to make sure that Ellie never annoyed or frustrated the player and that she remained a compelling entity throughout the game. Most importantly, we had to build a character that the player cared for.

Ellie is new to the world outside the military safe zone in which she grew up and new to the brutality and violence of the infected and humanity at large. She is seeing landscapes, cities, and actions as the player would, instead of through the world weary eyes of Joel. She is a young and fragile character in a dangerous world, and we wanted the AI to highlight this as well as support her growth and strength later in the game.

3.2 Starting from Scratch

The first decision we had to make was to start from scratch with just a few months of development remaining. Five months before we shipped, we had to present a press demo of the game, a combat encounter through a tight environment with a dozen or so infected. We wanted it to showcase how tense it would be fighting the infected and how having buddies with you would both aid you and increase the emotional impact of an encounter.

At that time, the two buddies in the encounter, Tess and Ellie, exhibited all the negative traits of buddy AI that we were trying to avoid: positioning themselves awkwardly, shooting at the wrong time, and generally getting underfoot. To avoid this, they had to be scripted for the entire duration, explained away using the video game trope of "staying back." Doing this completely removed them from the encounter and the player's attention; it was clear this was an unacceptable approach.

3.2.1 The Plan

The first thing we decided on was to keep buddies really close to the player. If a buddy is close to the player character, she is less likely to run into problems with enemy AI. Additionally, if she is far away from the player, she is easily forgotten, and the player will feel alone in the world, which is contrary to our storytelling goals for the game.

Once she reliably stayed close to the player, we started to give her utility in the form of both noncombat and combat behaviors. With these in place, she no longer felt like an escort quest. If she helps the player out of a tight situation, then the player feels thankful, grows to appreciate her presence, and has an improved opinion of the game in general.

Finally, we added touches to make her an interesting character, with a progression of combat vocalizations, a library of ambient animations for her to play, and a suite of noncombat conversation tracks. These systems are driven by the content creators, and with minimal effort, a character can become much more engaging.

3.2.2 Approach

One extremely important aspect of the development was how we thought about Ellie and the other buddies. We always treated her as an actual human being and spent time trying to get into her head, reasoning what she would do in a given situation and why. We tried to avoid the "gamification" of her AI as much as possible, restricting ourselves from cheating or doing things that would seem inhuman. We grew to genuinely care for Ellie and her well-being.

The decision to avoid cheating was extremely important. It's easy to cut corners by cheating, but even if the player never notices, it still moves you away from creating a living, breathing character, which was completely at odds with our goals for Ellie. There were exceptions, but we stuck to this policy as much as we possibly could.

3.3 Ambient Following

There are a lot of reasons for keeping a buddy character close to the player. Primarily, if she is sharing the same space as and behaving similarly to the player, then her actions can by definition be no more stupid than what the player is doing. If she has positioned herself

correctly and is still seen by an enemy, then the player will have been seen too and consequently will attribute the failure to themselves rather than the buddy.

Additionally, a buddy that is close to the player has increased opportunity to trigger relevant dialogue. This dialogue can both serve as character exposition and provide gameplay utility. For example, rather than having the buddy run out from hiding next to the player when she is about to be seen by an enemy, she can vocalize the threat and allow the player to handle it. We can also vocalize exclamations of surprise or good fortune, augmenting the tension and reward of an encounter.

In the context of *The Last of Us*, when the player is separated from Ellie and no longer has her vocalizations of danger to rely on, the encounter becomes increasingly tense, and consequently, the relationship with the buddy is strengthened.

3.3.1 Follow Positions

To enable a buddy character to follow the player, or another character, we created a follow system that generated and evaluated positions near the leading character, and then moved the buddy there elegantly. The core of this was a follow region, a torus around the leader described by a set of parameters provided in data.

A number of candidate follow positions were generated inside this follow region and then evaluated for quality. The generation of the candidate follow positions was done by casting three sets of navmesh rays, as shown in Figure 3.1.

A first set of rays fan out from the leader position to the follow region in order to make sure that there is a clear line of movement from the buddy to the player. One candidate follow position is generated for each ray that reaches the follow region; see Figure 3.1a.

A second set of rays are then cast forward from each candidate position to make sure the position isn't facing a wall (Figure 3.1b). We tried allowing positions that would be close to a wall and just had the character face away from the wall, but in practice, a buddy moving right next to a wall feels unnatural.

Finally, rays are cast from the player's location to each "forward" location, to ensure that movement forward from this location wouldn't put an obstacle between the player and the buddy (Figure 3.1c). This ray may seem unnecessary, but in testing, we found that

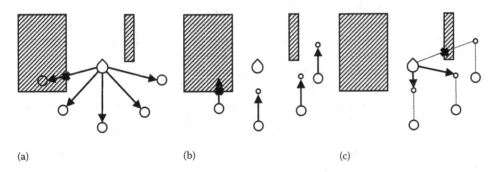

(a)   (b)   (c)

Figure 3.1

The generation of follow positions by casting a set of pathfinding raycasts. (a) Cast rays to generate candidate positions. (b) Cast rays to check forward direction. (c) Cast rays to check future position.

without it, Ellie would choose to stand on the other side of a doorway or fence. Adding this ray gave her a desire to stand in the same "room" as the player.

The resulting follow positions are then rated every frame, and an optimal position is chosen for the buddy to move to. These ratings are based on a number of criteria including

- Distance to the leader
- Staying on the same side of the leader
- Visibility of potential targets (either hiding or exposing)
- Not being in front of the player
- Distance to other buddies

3.3.2 Moving

Once we had chosen a position to move the buddy toward, we had to make sure she would perform the movement in a believable manner. We would watch her follow the player around a space, and if we saw a movement that seemed unnecessary or unnatural, we would pause the game and start investigating the cause.

From this, a lot of filters were added to the movement to make it appear more intelligent. First, we limited short-distance moves, only allowing them if they were absolutely necessary, for example, if her current location was exposed by an enemy. Then we prevented her from running past the leader character if possible, unless not doing so meant stopping in an undesirable location. It appeared very forced if she picked a follow position on the opposite side of the player and mechanically ran past the player. Allowing her to get "close enough" to her follow position, and not crowd the player, gave her follow behavior a very organic feel rather than the rigid behavior she had before.

Of course most of the time we are not generating follow positions around a stationary leader, as the player will be moving around the environment too. As the player moves, both the follow region and the generated follow positions move too. We regenerate follow positions each frame, but we include criteria in the position ratings to try and smooth out any noise.

In an ambient environment where the player is casually exploring a place, Ellie is allowed to saunter after the player without much urgency, while during combat, we like to keep her very close to the player. This meant creating a mapping from the desired movement distance to the buddy's movement speed to allow us to specify how urgently the buddy should move to her follow position. For short distances, a walk is sufficient; for extremely long distances, she must sprint; and in between, she may run.

Each movement mode (walk, run, and sprint) had a single fixed speed, which varied across buddies and was different from the player's movement speed. This meant that when following the player, she would approach some ideal distance from him and then oscillate between running and walking, which was clearly unnatural. To prevent this, we allowed the buddy to scale her movement animation speeds by as much as 25%, allowing her to stay in a given movement mode for longer. As she neared the threshold to start walking, she would scale back the speed of her run.

3.3.3 Dodging

We made the decision to have buddies not explicitly move out of the way of the player if they were there first. If the player and a buddy character are both stationary, we find that the player is not typically inclined to run straight at her, just as you would not run straight at a real-life friend standing near you. Instead of preemptively making her move, we assume the player is going to try and go around her and only at the last second make her play a canned animation dodging out of the way (along with a vocalization admonishing the player for encroaching on her personal space). This approach to dodging took what can frequently be a really frustrating and unrealistic behavior and turned it into a character element, making the player subconsciously respect Ellie and her choices.

3.3.4 Teleportation

One popular method to keep buddy characters near a player is teleportation, which can be effective but has a number of downsides. We decided very early on to never teleport the buddies for the purpose of keeping them near the player.

There were a number of reasons for this. The audio department didn't want the buddy's footsteps to suddenly appear closer to the player. We also didn't want to have situations where you know that Ellie is on one side of you and then suddenly she's on the other with no explanation for how she got there. You can write robust checks against this sort of issue, but if the player gets even a hint that teleportation is happening, it feels a little strange and can break the suspension of disbelief. We also just wanted to avoid it on principle, believing that if we aimed to make Ellie keep up with the player in all situations, then the end result would be more robust and believable. When we avoid cheating, we are forced to address the situations where we might cheat in a realistic way, and this creates small details in the character's behavior that make Ellie feel like a living, breathing character who is grounded in the world in which you are both participating.

Ultimately, the only time a buddy will teleport is when they need to immediately aid the player with a melee struggle, which is discussed later. We also considered allowing teleportation to bring Ellie closer to the player in cases where she was sufficiently far away, but in practice, this was rarely necessary.

3.4 Taking Cover

The follow system described earlier was largely used for ambient (i.e., noncombat) situations. Combat following, and particularly cover selection, requires something slightly different.

The Last of Us is a cover-based third-person game, so it was necessary to have the buddy characters take cover with the player efficiently. Our tools create "cover action packs" that represent places an AI character can take cover against a wall or similar obstacle, but ultimately this representation was too coarse for our needs. While enemy NPCs only require sparse information about where they can take cover, the player can take cover anywhere in the world. If we were going to keep the buddy characters nearby, then they needed to have the same ability.

3.4.1 Runtime Cover Generation

We used a hybrid approach to generate runtime cover, combining the system used by the NPCs with the dynamic system used by the player. We already have "cover edge" features generated by our tools, which are used to create the cover action packs that the enemy AI uses. These simply represent the intersection of a wall and floor collision plane, with a markup to indicate height and cornering.

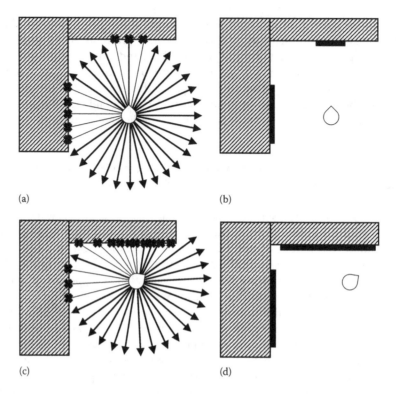

(a)

(b)

(c)

(d)

Figure 3.2

Generation of procedural cover edge features using collision raycasts. (a) Fire rays to find nearby collision. (b) Combine similar collision points to form cover edge features. (c) Fire rays again, when the leader moves. (d) Combine collision points with previous cover edge features to create larger edges.

To generate the runtime cover, first, we scan the environment around us and look for nearby cover edge features. We then augment this with a set of procedurally generated cover edge features. We cast a fan of raycasts from the leader's position against the collision geometry (see Figure 3.2a), compare the normal of the collision plane and location of each hit point, and then combine nearby points with a similar normal into procedural cover edge features (Figure 3.2b).

These two sets of cover edge features, one static and one procedural, are then combined and cached for future use. As the leader character moves, we perform the same tests (Figure 3.2c, d) and combine the results with the previous results. We only evict cover edge features from this cache when we start running out of storage. This combined set of cover edge features benefits from both the information derived by the tools and the runtime features, creating a more accurate set than either method alone. Unfortunately, the process was very computationally expensive, so doing it for all characters was unfeasible, and we had restrict it to just the buddy NPCs.

This set of cover edges is then rated to choose an ideal edge on which the buddy character should take cover. A large amount of time went into generating and tweaking the set of rating functions for cover edges, the most important being

- Visibility to enemies, a dot-product check
- Proximity to leader
- Predicted future visibility, derived by projecting enemy movement

3.4.2 Cover Share

Originally, the player was unable to share cover with a buddy; in fact, if the buddy saw the player approaching, she would pop out of cover, assuming that the player wanted to be in that location. This removed intentionality from the buddy's movement, much in the same way as dodging would, as discussed earlier. In order to solve this, we created an animation set in which Joel was able to enter cover on top of a buddy character, placing his hand on the wall next to her and shielding her with his body. The player was able to perform all the normal actions such as shooting or moving, and we didn't need to move the buddy at all.

One time, because of a bug, Ellie entered cover through Joel into this shared cover state. We realized it looked really believable, and with some small modifications to the animation set, we made it work all the time, allowing Ellie to take cover exactly where the player was.

We also added special dialogue lines, so the buddy character would comment on recent combat while sharing cover with the player. This cover share system really enhanced the bond with Ellie. It took our "stick close to the player" mantra to its logical conclusion, and it was virtually impossible as a player not to feel some compassion for Ellie when in cover share.

3.5 Combat Utility

Once we had the buddies following the player as robustly and smoothly as possible, it was time to move on to make them useful in combat. We always wanted Ellie and the other buddies to explicitly support the player rather than go off and do their own fighting. There were a number of ideals that drove our development of the buddy combat utility.

The game's difficulty was very carefully balanced, and we wanted to ensure the buddy performed consistently in a given encounter so that they wouldn't upset this balance. In particular, we didn't ever want a buddy to overpower an encounter and make the player feel useless. It was also important to make sure that the player saw the buddies doing things in combat. This is true of all AI characters but particularly so for buddies; they can be the most intelligent AI ever created, but if the player doesn't see what they are doing, then it is wasted effort.

There are also large sections of the game where Ellie is unarmed, but she still needs to interact in combat and support the player. This is where we started our development of combat behaviors.

3.5.1 Throwing

One of the most visceral combat actions Ellie performs is when she throws a brick at an approaching enemy. The logic to decide when to throw is very simple; we need to make sure that she isn't giving away the player's location but that she still throws the brick promptly enough to be effective. One of the primary triggers for the throw action is driven by hooking into the enemy perception and movement systems and predicting if they will be able to see the player in the near future.

These thrown objects stun the target for a few seconds, allowing the player to follow up in a number of ways: running away, melee attacking the enemy, grappling, etc. The throw action is put on a really long timer, to ensure it doesn't get overused. We always want it to be special and memorable when such an action occurs.

3.5.2 Grapples

Next, we added melee grapples, allowing an enemy to target and grab a buddy character. This was largely done through data by design, thanks to a verbose melee scripting system. We originally required the player to save Ellie every time she was grappled, but this quickly became tedious and clearly tipped us toward the "escort quest" design we were trying to avoid. Instead, we gave her a suite of animations allowing her to escape the grapple herself, after which she would reposition away from the temporarily stunned enemy, and we would disallow her from being targeted again for 15–30 s.

We kept the requirement for the player to save her in certain situations, but it was always done intentionally and infrequently. We would make sure she was visible and easily accessible to the player and that the player wasn't currently grappled himself. We wanted the player to want to protect Ellie, just not so often that it was irritating.

We also implemented the reverse situation; sometimes the player is grabbed by an enemy, and buddy characters are able to save you. People tend to feel really grateful if Ellie stabs a guy who has them in a headlock; this can take a desperate situation and turn the tables.

As mentioned earlier in this chapter, grapples are the only time we allow teleportation of a buddy. We decided that if the player is being grappled and we want Ellie to save them, then it's an acceptable time to teleport. During the grapple, the player has no camera control, so we can ensure it is facing in a direction that does not reveal the teleport.

3.5.3 Gifting

We already had one scripted sequence where one of the buddies, David, gave the player a box of ammo while fighting off infected at the start of the Winter chapter. Players reacted so well to this that we felt it should be something systematic that Ellie could do.

The game uses a complex drop system that works out what supplies should spawn in an area and what dead bodies should drop, and we just hooked straight into this to figure out what Ellie should give the player. We restricted it to ammo and health packs, meaning that the player would still need to scavenge for crafting items to apply as weapon upgrades. Because it was tied directly into the existing system, it didn't change the difficulty balancing that had already occurred, despite coming online very late in development.

We added another really long timer to her gifting, to prevent annoying the player. In the first playtest that we ran with gifting enabled, we noticed one player was stuck in a particular spot, and Ellie would give him ammo every minute. It not only highlighted that the level design needed some fixing, but it devalued the act of gifting. When properly tuned, it really helped to enhance the bond between her and the player; she would whisper and hand you something useful at exactly the right times.

3.6 Armed Combat

Having an extensive suite of unarmed combat behaviors, it was time to focus on making Ellie use a gun effectively and believably. For positioning, we used both the procedural cover edge features and the follow positions discussed earlier. Again we stuck with our mantra of staying near the player, and the settings for generation of follow positions were tuned to bring her closer to the player and allow her to move more responsively.

For the most part, we would try and mirror the player's decisions, crouching and taking cover or standing upright and out in the open in conjunction with the player's character. When in doubt, we would always prefer to select a cover location, as that was rarely a bad place to be.

Initially, we planned for the adult buddies like Tess and Bill to operate more independently in the environment, but in practice, it always felt like they were abandoning the player, and we didn't want that. Instead, they all behave like Ellie, although with more relaxed parameters for positioning and movement.

3.6.1 Shooting

The game heavily emphasizes stealth, so having a buddy give away your location is extremely infuriating and breaks all of the trust that the buddy has gained. Thus, knowing when (and when not) to shoot is absolutely key.

The first thing we did was reverse the logic for shooting; instead of being happy to shoot most of the time—like the enemy NPCs—Ellie wants to not shoot. This not only makes sense for AI reasons but also for real-world reasons; she is a young girl and hesitant to use a gun. We then built logic to give her permission to fire.

If the player is actively firing a weapon or engaging in noisy melee combat, then Ellie is allowed to fire upon her target. In addition, we model the intentions of enemy NPCs and allow her to fire if the player is in immediate danger. Finally, if the player was trying to sneak away from an encounter, we tried to recognize this by comparing the player's location with the enemy NPC's perception of where the player was. If these were significantly different, then we considered the player to be back in stealth, and shooting would no longer be allowed.

3.6.2 Balancing

After we enabled gun usage, suddenly Ellie was a killing machine. She did the same damage as the player and was pretty accurate. Fortunately, we had a lot of knobs to control her damage output: damage values, accuracy, firing rate, and so on.

We didn't want to change damage, because that makes an NPC feel broken. If it takes the player three shots to down an enemy, it should take the buddy the same number of shots (with some small margin of error). We also didn't want to change the fire rate or accuracy too much. That would make her face down an enemy with her gun pointing at it and shoot so infrequently or inefficiently that again she felt broken. We made minor changes to fire rate and accuracy to bring them to a believable limit on a per encounter basis, but the buddies were still far too effective.

In order to address this, we decided that if the player isn't going to see the hit, then it isn't necessary for a buddy to do any damage. This meant the player would hear a normal burst of gunshots, but the composition of the encounter didn't change. In practice, players rarely realized that the buddy wasn't doing any damage, so we were able to retain game balance without breaking the player's immersion in the game.

With that said, we didn't want Ellie to feel completely useless, so we tried to identify key moments when it would be good for her to hit and damage a target. In particular, if the player hasn't seen her shoot anyone recently, or if the player is in immediate danger from a charging enemy, low health, a grapple, or something similar, then this is a good time for Ellie's shots to start landing.

Despite all of these changes, we still found the need to lower her fire rate below "realistic" levels to balance damage, so we gave her a "furtive" idle animation that makes her look nervous when she wasn't shooting. This really helped pad out the gaps between shots, and the animation also helped to build her character.

3.6.3 Cheating

Throughout development, there was one prominent decision that we had to make: specifically, whether or not enemies could see Ellie and be alerted by her. For the majority of development, they were able to see her, and this drove us to make her as stealthy as possible, perfecting the AI as much as we could. In practice, it worked about 90%–95% of the time, and we were very proud of how close we got to perfect buddy stealth, but ultimately we had to make a decision one way or the other. Neither option was ideal: either buddies would occasionally give away the player's location, or enemies would never be able to see buddies unless they were actively in combat.

In the end, we decided that the only viable option was to make buddies invisible to enemy NPCs if the player was being stealthy. The result is that sometimes a buddy will run past a bad guy in clear view and not be seen, but as discussed, we had done a lot of work to make sure this wouldn't happen frequently. It breaks realism but considers the alternative. If Ellie was seen even once and gave away the player's location, then the bond between them would become fractured, and we wanted to avoid that at all costs.

3.7 Finishing Touches

Having a robust, well balanced, and ultimately fun buddy AI up and running, it was finally time to add the little touches that would really make Ellie and the other buddies come alive. It's important to recognize that much of what makes a character really deep and compelling has nothing to do with AI; it is having a large library of content to draw from.

3.7.1 Vocalizations

We realized very early on that there needed to be close integration between the combat AI and the dialogue system. This enabled us to easily have a buddy comment on specifics of the recent combat, such as the types of kill she had witnessed or if she had saved you during the fight.

Completely by coincidence, we noticed that Ellie's vocalizations would frequently mirror what the player was exclaiming. After a particularly gruesome battle, it wouldn't be uncommon for the player to utter profanities, followed shortly by Ellie playing an identical vocalization. This made an entirely unplanned connection between the player and Ellie.

3.7.2 Callouts

Next, we added callouts of unseen threats, either whispered or yelled depending on the severity of the situation. This system tries to model the player's view of the world and keep track of threats that they aren't aware of, and will then have a buddy comment on the threat at an appropriate time.

One very important thing we discovered when testing this new callout system is that it is absolutely imperative to ensure that whenever a buddy calls out an enemy, the enemy is there for the player to see. We were a little overzealous with our callouts originally, and Ellie would call out someone who she had only just caught a glimpse of or who may have ducked behind a wall again. When the player heard her warn about an enemy that they were unable to spot, it reflected badly on Ellie's intelligence, so we iterated hard to eliminate bad callouts. This is a classic example of a situation where the requirements for AI are actually more stringent than they would be for human intelligence.

When the system was working and tuned, it really helped give the player a better view of the world. We had a pretty minimal HUD—no minimap in the corner showing enemy locations—so any additional information you could get about the encounter was invaluable. Ellie was acting as an information source for the player, and it really improved the bond.

3.7.3 Ambience

Huge portions of the game have no combat, and we needed Ellie to be interesting and alive during these sections. There are lots of scripted dialogue interactions with the player, of which some are explicitly triggered through the controller and others are triggered dynamically after combat encounters.

We also created a suite of idle animations for her to play, things as simple as cleaning her knife, tying her shoelace, or straightening her hair. Fortunately, it was really easy for animators to get content like this into the game.

Finally, we added an "explore" system for buddies where designers would instrument the world with points of interest and cinematic interactions for her to use. The designers loved this and very quickly made the open spaces a lot livelier with buddies searching them, looking in cabinets, and so on. It's a really basic system, it only took a day or so to implement, but it felt great going into a space and having Ellie start wandering off looking at things. She shared in the player's wonderment at this abandoned world. We got a lot of good feedback about the sections where Ellie would explore, and designers loved having this tool to flesh out their spaces.

3.8 Conclusion

After all of this, buddy AI in *The Last of Us* was a complete success and really enhanced the game. Our hard work paid off and strengthened the bond between Ellie and the player, and the half dozen additional buddy characters that the player encounters throughout the game are unique and believable entities in the world.

Just 5 months of development from a very small team—just one core engineer with backup from the rest of the character engineering team—meant that we had to have laser focus on what we needed to accomplish. We learned that the key to good buddy AI development and AI development, in general, does not lie in the complexity of the systems driving it but in the nuances of the character performance.

Getting into the right mindset was absolutely key for this. It sounds clichéd, but from day one, we tried to approach Ellie's character, and all the other buddies, as living, breathing characters in a world we were creating. Trying to empathize with their situation and reason about how they would operate in this world was central to everything we did.

The core of Ellie's AI is a robust and believable following system. Even before Ellie was able to shoot or do anything in combat, she felt great just by moving intelligently, taking cover in good locations, and staying out of the player's way. After that was in place, we did everything possible to eliminate the traditional annoyances associated with buddy characters, coupled with giving her agency in the world through her combat abilities.

The majority of the development time was spent on iteration, rather than building new systems. We had an almost manic obsession with fine-tuning the details of follow positioning, firing parameters, and ambient dialogue triggers. Having the tools available to iterate on and debug AI is absolutely essential, and it enabled prototyping new behaviors and tweaking things as we were watching them.

Another key to success was to put the buddies' combat abilities behind really big timers. In a long game, you don't want to tire the player out with witty banter, overzealous gifting, or special moves. If Ellie saved you from a melee grapple just once during the game, you would remember that moment fondly and talk about it. If she gave you a health pack around every corner, you wouldn't think of her as helpful, but it would become just another pickup, devaluing the act and her presence.

Finally, making the decision that a buddy would never break stealth was an extremely important one to make. Ultimately, we are making a game here, and your buddy AI can be as intelligent or realistic as possible, but if they ruin what the player is trying to do just once, it's all in vain.

Realizing NPCs
Animation and Behavior Control for Believable Characters

Jeet Shroff

4.1 Introduction

A core goal for game developers is to build nonplayer characters (NPCs) that are believable to the player. Believability does not necessarily imply realism, but in order to be believable, these characters must move convincingly, bound by their physicality and environment. They must look, act, and react meaningfully, both individually and in groups. Their actions and intentions must be clearly understood by the player. NPCs that maintain the illusion of believability compel the player to interact with them, further sell the fantasy, and ground the player within the game world. The process of clearly visualizing and communicating not only the NPCs' actions but also their intentions can be referred to as behavior realization.

Animation plays a central role in bringing NPC behaviors to life. By focusing on realizing NPC behaviors with improved animation fidelity, in combination with systems that help control how behaviors are varied, assigned, and executed by NPCs, we can ensure the authenticity of our characters.

This chapter will discuss a wide range of animation techniques that can be used to provide improved realization of NPC behaviors while simultaneously addressing the cost of production and memory budgets. In addition, it will look at ways to control the execution of behaviors in an effort to provide the player with a consistently positive and believable experience.

4.2 Character Movement

Nearly all NPCs have to be able to move in some way. Believable movement does its best to respect the laws of motion, factoring in inertia and momentum. In addition, characters that play animations that convey their intention while moving increase their authenticity by providing the player an awareness of their mental state and context. In this section, we will look at a few techniques to help accomplish this while still keeping our memory and production costs low.

4.2.1 Movement Models

Many game engines use a game-driven approach to character movement, where the animation does not define the motion of the character. Instead, movement is driven by an AI controller that evaluates the position of the character and requests the physics system to move the character's physical representation. The controller also feeds this information to the animation system, which plays animations that match the movement. For example, if the AI controller wishes to move the character forward, a forward moving walk or run animation might be selected by the animation system. Such animations would be authored as moving on-spot animations. This is a fully game-driven approach to character movement.

The alternative is to allow the animation to drive the character's movement. This is referred to as animation-driven movement and is achieved through the use of a *root* or *reference node* within the character's skeleton. The root node is a bone that represents the translation and rotation of the character's motion during the animation. The animation contains transform data for this bone for each frame of animation, just like it does for every other bone. This node is generally placed on the ground, centered directly under the hips of the character, as shown in Figure 4.1.

Every frame, after updating the animation pose, the position and orientation of the root node is passed to the physics system, which updates the position and orientation of the character's capsule (as shown in Figure 4.2). This is referred to as "extracting motion from the animation."

Both these techniques have their advantages. Game-driven movement provides us with maximum level of flexibility as it drives the character independent of animation. Animation-driven movement ensures that the character's overall motion matches that of the animation, providing the best visual results. In addition, this approach better conveys a character's change in momentum along with intention of motion when necessary. For example, a well-authored transition animation that drives the character fully through animation can convey the energy and acceleration or deceleration needed for the character

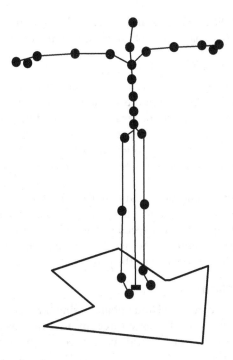

Figure 4.1

The arrow represents the root node and where it lies in the hierarchy of the rig.

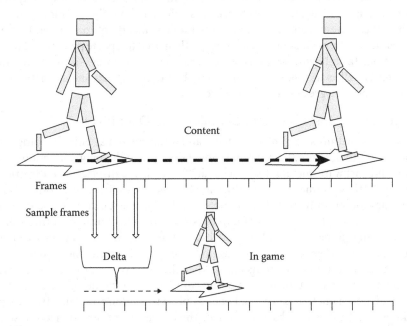

Figure 4.2

Motion extraction of the root node.

during such movement. Effective realization requires both control and fidelity, which we can achieve through a combination of both of these techniques.

4.2.2 Decoupling Extracted Motion

When combining game- and animation-driven movement, it is important to ensure that the extracted motion is decoupled from the animation update. In other words, instead of directly updating physics (and the character's capsule) with the animation's motion when the animation pose is updated, we can separate the animation from the motion update. This allows us to modify the extracted motion in order to better control the character and also to increase animation coverage (i.e., to cover a wider range of motion using a given animation set).

We want to limit our modifications and base them on the original extracted motion. This avoids visual inconsistencies (such as keeping our characters from significantly sliding when moving) and also preserves specific movement characteristics such as weight and energy. In other words, it allows us to stay true to the intentions of the animation and to avoid changes that might be noticed by the player.

4.2.3 Motion Correction

Character motion can be represented and updated using three core components: the displacement direction (i.e., the world space direction that the character is moving), the orientation of the character (i.e., the world space direction that the character is facing), and the speed at which the character is moving. Each frame, after the motion has been extracted, the change in displacement direction, orientation, and speed is read and applied to our character's physical representation by passing that information to the physics system. If no change is made, then the character is being driven fully via animation.

Each of these components can be corrected independently of each other, to match a specific game situation. This corrected change is then used to update physics and the character's motion. The following sections will describe a variety of ways in which we can correct motion as well as techniques that use a combination of game- and animation-driven movement to provide greater animation coverage.

4.2.4 Correcting Displacement Direction and Orientation

The animations within a movement system can be categorized as either looping, transition, or one-off (nonlooping) animations. Some examples of looping animations include forward- and backward-moving (or "backpedal") cycles. The displacement direction and orientation for these animations typically remain at the same offset to each other throughout the course of the animation. For example, the displacement direction and orientation in a looping backpedal animation point in opposite directions throughout the entire animation. Looping animations are also created so that the start and end frames are identical, so that you can play them over and over again to make the character move continuously.

In contrast, transition animations may update the offset of the displacement direction and orientation throughout the course of the animation to account for the change in the transition of movement that is needed. For example, a transition animation from standing to walking might rotate the character to face the displacement direction and also move and accelerate the character in that direction. Looping, transition, and one-off animations can all use motion correction to extend their coverage.

4.2.4.1 Looping Animations

The displacement direction and orientation of looping animations can be corrected to match a target direction. The target direction is set up by the path following or movement controller. In the case of following a path facing forward, the character will need to align their displacement direction and orientation to be along the path, so that they do not veer off the path or unintentionally strafe sideways.

A wide range of smoothing algorithms can be used to drive the orientation and displacement direction toward the one needed by the path. The most basic approach would be to use a simple interpolation. On analyzing the path, every frame, the controller sets up the target directions that are needed. Then new directions are evaluated that smoothly drive the current directions to the targets. These directions are passed on to physics. Other algorithms that factor in angular acceleration, along with the curvature of the path, can be used to provide more believable results. For example, we can use sets of tunable acceleration curves to control the rate of correction of the character's displacement direction and orientation for different circumstances. The speed of the character must also be modified to account for the radius of the turn (as shown in Figure 4.3), but speed adjustments will be discussed in a later section. Since the animation is updated independently of the corrected motion, we can add a procedural lean to account for these corrections and visually communicate this change to the player.

In order to be able to correct the displacement direction and orientation of our animations, we must impose certain constraints on the way the root node is animated. In the case of these looping animations, the animations should be animated within one plane (such as the XZ plane; in our examples we will always assume that Y is up). In addition, we

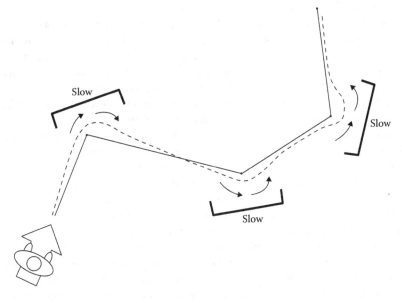

Figure 4.3

Following a path while facing forward using motion correction.

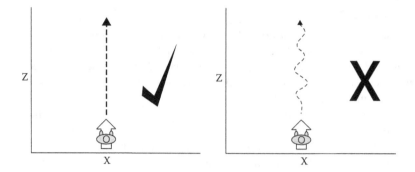

Figure 4.4

Root node motion for cyclical movement animations.

also need to minimize the curvature within the translation for the root node, as shown in Figure 4.4. Transition animations require a different set of constraints.

4.2.4.2 Transition and One-Off Animations

Transition animations, such as starting to move, planting to turn, and stop animations help to communicate a character's change in momentum to the player. Using a naive approach, we often need a wide range of animations to cover all cases. For example, a given starting to move animation can only rotate a character by a fixed amount. Blending animations together may help to alleviate the amount of coverage needed, but persistently blending motion-based animations can lose the subtle nuances of motion particularly authored for specific directions. Motion correction can be used in this case to generate a wider range of coverage while preserving the fidelity of the original content.

Let us continue with the example of starting to move. When starting to move from an idle, we want the character to be able to move in any direction without getting stuck in the transition animation for too long. To account for this, we can use motion correction to perform an additional rotation after the orientation is calculated from the extracted motion. This correction adjusts for the difference between rotation in the animation and the rotation required to face the target direction, which is fixed in this case. On each frame, we add the appropriate portion of this difference as a delta to the animation rotation to ensure that the character ends up facing the intended direction. When using this approach, it is important to ensure that the animation is built with a little shuffling or movement in both feet. This helps to hide the fact that the feet will slide as the character turns. Ensuring that the difference is spread evenly across every frame of the rotational component of the animation and imposing a constraint that the root node be rotated at a constant rate during the animation, we can also help to minimize the sliding that one might notice.

Using this approach, we were able to create 360° of coverage using just three start animations: a 0° direction, a 120° to the right direction, and a 120° to the left direction. This provided surprisingly good results, even though we might think more coverage would be necessary. With that said, if the fidelity is not good enough, more coverage can easily be added by adding just a few more transitions (for instance, 60° to the right and left transitions). This is illustrated in Figure 4.5.

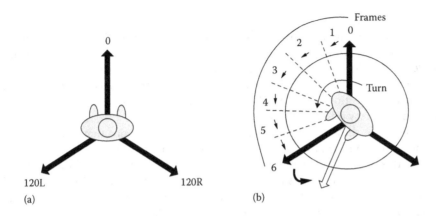

Figure 4.5

Motion correction applied during starting to move animations. (a) Original start animations, 0, 120R, and 120L. (b) Intended angle in white is 155L. Select the 120L animation, add on the difference of 35 degrees, and spread uniformly across the 6 frames of rotation to end up at 155 degrees from the original facing angle at the end of the rotation.

As each of our three components can be updated independently, it is worth noting that in this case, the displacement direction can be corrected as described in the previous section via the controller, the speed can be fully driven by the animation, and the orientation can be corrected using the aforementioned technique. Within the same animation, toward the end of the rotational segment, the orientation can be blended to be corrected by the same smoothing technique used in looping animations to match the requested direction. In cases where target direction is varying during the course of the animation, we can use a combined technique of orientation smoothing along with the delta rotational adjustment per frame. Different combinations of either movement model with motion correction can be used for many forms of transition animations, such as stop animations or plant and turn animations, as well as one-off animations such as rotating or reacting in place animations.

Displacement direction or orientation correction can also be used to add variety to the trajectory of one-off animations such as a hit reaction or death animations from an explosion. In the case of explosion animations, we can also add a random upward component to the extracted motion, which changes how high the character's body flies. As with the orientation changes described earlier, the upward component should be distributed across the course of the animation. All of these techniques can create variety and increase coverage from a small set of animations.

Finally, motion correction can also be applied to one-off animations where the end position of the character is set by the game. This can be used for animations like entering a vehicle or interacting with a specific object. As with the adjustment on the start animations, we can calculate the difference between the end position of the one-off animation and the intended target position and then apply an appropriate-sized delta, each frame, to align the character's displacement direction and orientation accordingly. Speed adjustments can also be made to match this correction.

4.2.5 Correcting Speed

Looping animations are typically authored to have a fixed speed throughout the animation. As mentioned earlier, in some cases, we may want to temporarily alter that speed. For example, when following a path, we might want to slow the character down as he or she goes around a tight turn. Similarly, we might want to alter the speed of the player character to match the position of the thumb stick. We want to do this without creating custom animations for every possible speed.

One approach, shown in Figure 4.6, is to take two animations that were authored at different speeds and blend them together in order to achieve the desired result. While common, this approach can impose restrictions on the authoring of the animations themselves and typically results in a loss of animation fidelity. In reality, moving at different speeds introduces a wide range of subtleties in body movement and stride (distance between each step) of a character. In order to ensure that these cycles blend well with each other, these differences usually have to be heavily dampened or eliminated. In addition, in most cases, these animations need to be authored with the same number of steps, which is limiting both from a stylistic and a motion capture perspective. The bottom line is that the subtleties of motion are lost during the persistent blend of all these animations. Another approach is to drive the character's speed through the game, while correcting the animation's playback rate to match this speed. This maintains the original posing, weight, and motion of the character from the source animation. By limiting the correction to the

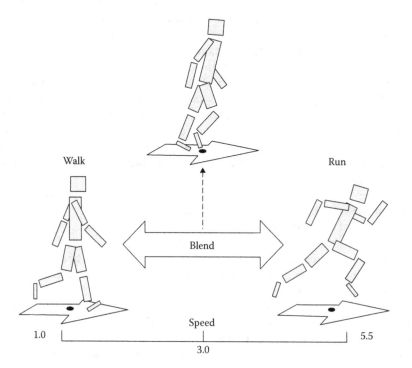

Figure 4.6

Blending animations together to create coverage for speed.

extracted motion and adjusting the playback rate of the animation to match the correction, we can satisfy both the fidelity and coverage concerns.

During gameplay, the target speed is calculated for the character each frame. If this speed is faster or slower than the current speed of the character, every frame, the AI controller calculates a "next" speed that approaches the target speed using smoothing or an acceleration/deceleration curve (similar to what we did for displacement direction and orientation). Since the motion is decoupled from the pose, we can pass this speed on to the physics system to move the character. At the same time, we visually match the speed of the character by adjusting their animation playback rates. As the character speeds up or slows down, we will need to transition between animations (e.g., from walk to run to sprint).

We control this by specifying a set of speed ranges. Each speed range specifies a looping animation that we have identified as a speed that our character typically moves at (i.e., their usual run speed, walk speed, sprint speed). The speeds of these animations become our *reference speeds*. The animation is then played back at a lower or higher rate to account for the difference between the current speed and the reference speed. Since this is simply a visual match with decoupled motion, the reference speed for an animation can be adjusted, even if it doesn't really move at that speed in the animation, to best match the character's movement in game. To ensure smooth motion, we allow the speed ranges to overlap, so that there are transition areas where we change from one animation to another as the speed smoothly moves up or down to the next reference speed. Each frame, we check which animation or animations are appropriate given the current speed. If only one animation is appropriate, then that is what we play. When we are in a transition where two animations are appropriate, we blend them together. Note that this is the only time when these scaled animations are blended together. The amount of overlap is defined by the available coverage. This technique is illustrated in Figure 4.7.

We can minimize the amount of time that the character remains within an overlapping range by ensuring that the AI controller always tries to set the target speed to be a reference speed. This avoids the persistent blend and ensures that the character plays the core looping animation at the reference speed, as it was originally intended as much as possible. As the overlap between these ranges is fairly small, we rarely notice the difference in the actual movement and animation sampling.

Transition animations, such as start or stop transitions, can also be speed corrected to visually match the target speed of motion. In these cases, the speed is not constant throughout the animation, so specific reference speeds are defined for the varying acceleration and deceleration segments within the animation. Further improvement can be made by removing the need for the reference animations to have the same number of steps. This allows for more freedom when capturing and creating data. For example, a walk animation requires far more steps to look natural than a run, since the walk is at a much slower pace and begins to look mechanical when looped, while a highly intentional run is far more forgiving. In order to do this, we need two variants of the animation: the base version and a variant that is intended specifically for blending. When in an area of the speed range that overlaps, we play the blending variant, but as soon as we are out of the overlap range, we go back to the better-looking base version. We can use an animation technique known as pose matching (described later) to allow us to smoothly blend between the base version and the blending variant as needed.

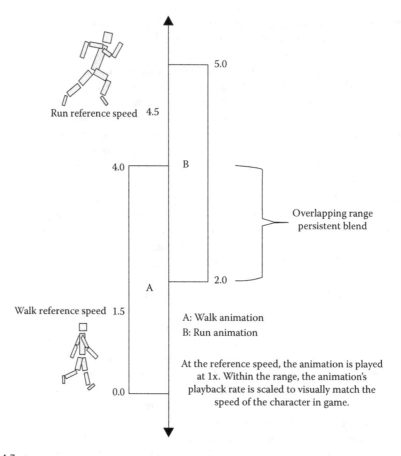

Run reference speed 4.5

5.0

4.0   B

Overlapping range
persistent blend

A

2.0

Walk reference speed 1.5

0.0

A: Walk animation

B: Run animation

At the reference speed, the animation is played
at 1x. Within the range, the animation's
playback rate is scaled to visually match the
speed of the character in game.

Figure 4.7

Using ranges to scale the playback rate of animations to visually match the character's
motion.

Using speed correction along with speed ranges can yield a higher level of quality while
still allowing for the smooth transitions that we can get by blending the transitions as we
speed up or slow down.

4.3 Interrupting and Blending Movement

One of the challenges when transitioning between moving animations is that if the time
between footfalls, or the motion of the arms, or some other significant feature in the
two animations is not precisely in sync, the character's appendages may scissor, freeze,
windmill, or otherwise move implausibly. For example, the time between footfalls when
running is generally longer than the time in between footfalls when walking. Thus, at
one second into a run animation, the right foot may be descending, headed toward a foot
plant. In the walk animation, the right foot may already have planted, and the left foot
may be swinging forward. If you try to blend these two animations simply based off of

time, you'll get odd results because the feet are doing different things. This is particularly common when we must interrupt an animation at any point.

4.3.1 Pose Matching

Pose matching is a technique that addresses this problem. Instead of blending animations based on elapsed time, we blend the two animations based on their pose. In most moving animations, the pose can be defined by phase. In this case, the phase of an animation is defined as the time in the swing cycle of each foot, as shown in Figure 4.8, going from 0 to 1. With that said, for any given set of animations, the definition used should depend on the feature that you are trying to match. Phase information can be generated offline and stored as metadata, keeping runtime calculations to a minimum.

States can define whether to apply pose matching when they blend in from another state or only when they blend out to another state. Looping animations, for instance, will choose to pose match when a character transitions to and from them, since they include phase information for the entire cycle. Certain transition animations, however, may only choose to apply pose matching when transitioning out of the state. This is necessary because pose matching on entry may cause us to skip the most important parts of the animation.

4.3.2 Pose-Only and Per-Bone Blending

Interrupting movement to come to a stop also poses a unique set of challenges. Stop animations are transitions that are used to convey the shift in momentum and deceleration needed when a character comes to a stop. Often, our games require that the characters come to a stop on a dime, especially when dealing with the player releasing game pad input. Stopping in an instant is an animator's nightmare. Coming to a complete stop immediately is both physically impossible and visually unnatural. This problem is exacerbated by the fact that if you're using motion capture, the data will

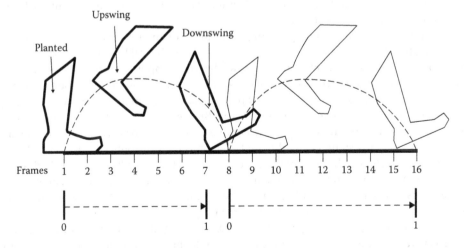

Figure 4.8

Phase match information, going from 0.0 to 1.0 with respective frames.

always have some motion in it. A simple animation technique that helps to improve the quality of this is pose-only blending.

When we transition from a movement animation to our stop animation, we can blend the pose and the root node separately. In the case of an instant stop, we do not include any of the root node translation, which ensures that the character will stop instantly, but we still blend in the pose from the movement animation, which helps to create the illusion of deceleration and alleviates the visual harshness of the sudden transition. In order to work, this requires that the root node for the stop animations be authored without any translation.

This idea can be further extended not just to blend the root node without any blending but also to blend different sets of bones at different rates. This is known as per-bone blending. Using this technique, we can create the illusion of momentum or motion lag, for example, by blending in the upper- and lower-body parts differently.

4.4 Combining Actions

NPCs often need to do more than one thing at the same time. For instance, they might need to carry and aim their weapons while running or talk on a cell phone while riding a bicycle. In the case of carrying or aiming weapons, having to create content for each different weapon type is also cumbersome and expensive. Memory limitations make this approach further challenging. In this section, we will discuss techniques for realizing these features using specific combat-based examples.

4.4.1 Animation Masking

Sharing animation data among features is a great way to save on animation memory. Animation masking is one way to do this. We can use bone masks to split animations into combinations of masked animations that can be recombined as needed. This allows us to ensure that there is never any duplication of animation data. Data that can be shared is exported out as a mask only once. This mask is then reused as needed. Masks should be generated offline. We can think of our final animation pose as being built at runtime from a combination of these bone masks.

Figure 4.9 demonstrates this idea using the example of an idle animation. The original idle animation can be thought of as using no mask, including all bones shown at the very top. However, as we build content to hold a two-handed weapon such as a rifle, we realize the upper-body portion of the animation needs to be different, but the lower-body portion of both of these animations is the same. So we mask the original animation into two: a lower-body mask (A) and an upper-body mask (B). We then share the lower-body mask for both animations and need only a rifle holding upper-body mask (C) to create the rifle holding idle. When a significantly different weapon type is introduced, such as an RPG, we only need to change the arms of the upper-body two-handed rifle mask (C). And so we further mask that to separate the arms into their respective masks (E) and (F), along with the armless upper-body animation (D) to account for the two different weapons. This allows us to minimize our use of animation memory.

We can further optimize this by masking out bones that do not require key frame data for every frame of the animation. These often include the face and finger bones. They can be exported as simple poses, so that we only include data for those animations that require their bones to move.

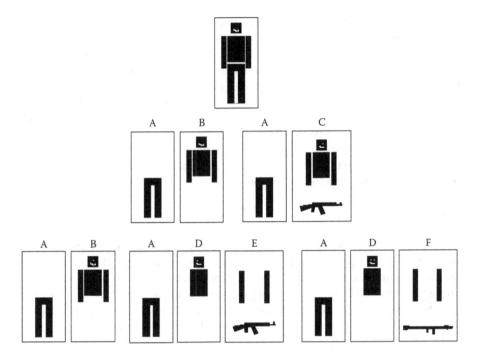

Figure 4.9

Masking animations for an idle with weapons.

4.4.2 Animation Mirroring

In order to save additional memory, we can make use of animation mirroring. Mirrored animations are animations that can be played symmetrically on either side of a plane, for example, animations that can be played either to the right or left, requiring the same movements in either direction (looping animations where the character is aiming either to the left or right side or one-off animations such as entering or exiting a vehicle from either side). Content is built only for one side and mirrored during runtime to get the coverage for the other side.

4.4.3 Animation Layering

Animation layering is a technique that can be used to play secondary actions that do not need to be synchronized with the base action. Animation layers can be thought of as tracks that can play an animation. You can think of the main layer as being the base animation that is played on the character. Once the base animation has been selected as either a no mask or combined with a set of masked animations, additional layers of animation that do not need to be synchronized with the base animation can be sequentially blended together with this pose to create the final pose of the character. When a layer's blend weight is 1.0, it means that the animation that is being played on that layer is completely overriding the animation on the layer beneath it. This is exactly what is needed when we want to play an animation that can cover and override multiple base animations. This saves us additional authoring time and memory.

For example, we could have an animation that uses a single arm to detonate an explosive or both arms to reload a weapon. This technique also works very well for things like facial animation and conversational gestures. These animations can generally be used across several base animation states. Animation data per layer are applied sequentially in the local space of the character. To ensure that these animations work well, we must enforce the bone masks to be flexible enough to be applied independently of the base animation state. We can do this by limiting the masks to head or arm-only animations, thus preserving the base pose as best as possible.

These techniques are not limited to weapons or combat alone. The important takeaway here is that when it comes to dealing with large feature sets, it is important to think of ways to reuse animation content as widely as possible.

4.5 Tracking

NPCs often need to be able to track another object—for instance, by looking at another wandering NPC or aligning a weapon to aim at a specific target. Furthermore, we often need our NPCs to be able to track an object in all directions. Tracking an object while aiming a weapon without breaking the original pose or sticking the weapon through any part of the character's body is a difficult problem to get right. In this section, using aiming as an example, we can look at some techniques to solve this problem.

4.5.1 Additive Aiming Poses

Additive animations are animations that are applied as additional offsets to an existing animation. These animations are created by taking the difference between two animations to generate offsets per frame. We can apply these offsets onto the base animation to generate a different pose. Many games use additives to provide extra runtime animation noise. This adds variety and communicates a character's context to the player, for instance, additional breathing when a character is tired or leaning when making a hard turn.

There are two different ways we can generate and apply additive offsets: either as additive pose offsets (as a single frame) or as additive animation offsets (animations that are synced with the original animation). In either case, these additive offsets are created offline.

When using additive pose offsets, we must specify the animation pose and a reference pose that we can use to generate the offsets for that pose. For example, in the case of a leaning pose additive, we would provide the maximum leaning pose as the animation pose and the straight pose as the reference pose. When we generate the additive pose offset for this, we would get the additive offsets necessary to add to the straight pose to create the maximum leaning pose. We should ensure that the additive animation pose is built directly from the reference pose. This ensures a controlled and high-fidelity final pose when applying the offsets at runtime.

Coming back to the example of aiming, animators can create aiming poses for the maximum angles needed for aiming. We then use a reference pose of the base animation to generate the offsets for each maximum angle. Finally, a persistent blend of these pose offsets is used at runtime to create the final pose with the weapon aimed correctly. We should make sure this blended additive is applied last within the animation blend tree.

This minimizes the adulteration of the pose. If further precision or fidelity is required, we can add more pose offsets at specific angles until we get the quality results that we need.

It is often a good idea to use this solution only for vertical aiming, that is, upward and downward, and instead to use inverse kinematics (IK) for our horizontal aiming. This dual aiming system will be discussed in greater detail later.

Additive pose offsets work exceptionally well for looping animations where the overall pose does not change significantly throughout the course of the base animation. Using additives for aiming provides the animator more control and allows the character to still hit key-authored poses, resulting in higher quality. In addition, using additive poses is a great way to minimize the amount of memory and time needed to create fully synced aiming animations for every base animation that would need to support aiming.

4.5.2 Additive Aiming Animations

The pose-based additive aiming solution does have a limitation. Additive pose offsets don't quite work when the pose itself changes significantly during the course of the base animation. An example of such an animation would be a hard landing animation from a long fall. Since there is a significant squash component during the beginning of the animation, followed by a stretch component after which the hips and head stabilize, we would require different offsets along the course of the animation to ensure that we maintain the intended aiming direction. To solve this problem, we can use synced additive animations that are authored at the required maximum aiming angles. We then can generate offsets frame by frame for the whole animation. As before, we then blend in a weighted offset to create the angles we need. This solution should only be used for animations that require it, because it requires significantly more memory. When it is required, we can decrease the memory requirements by only creating an additive pose for every X frames of the base animation (where X is typically something like 10) and apply the offsets accordingly. This still provides the animators enough control to create high-quality aiming offsets, while dramatically reducing the size of the additive animations.

4.5.3 Inverse Kinematics

Although we could use additives for both vertical and horizontal aiming, doing so would require a lot more poses to ensure coverage of every possible aim angle. In addition, it can limit the animators to altering only very specific sets of bones in each directional offset to ensure that they don't conflict with each other. Finally, if you need additive animations (rather than just poses), authoring the animations to meet these constraints can be painfully time-consuming.

As an alternative, IK works relatively well for horizontal aiming because the core rotation for aiming horizontally can be limited to a smaller set of bones. To make this work well, the locomotion system should select its movement animations based on the horizontal aiming range. Within a range, the horizontal aiming coverage needed is reasonably small and thus easily achievable through the use of IK. We can also choose to use a cheaper version of this for horizontal tracking when pointing or looking at an object. This rule generalizes that when using IK, it is important to select the right animations and bones to apply the IK to.

In addition to horizontal tracking, we use IK in other situations such as a postprocessing for foot or hand placement and for adding procedural variation to the pose.

4.6 Behaviors

The animation techniques described previously increase the fidelity of character realization of each individual NPC. However, maintaining the believability of our world requires us to think beyond that, looking at how often a character executes a specific behavior, how varied it is, and how it is distributed across multiple NPCs.

4.6.1 Creating Variety

Too often in games, we see an NPC play the same animations or behavior over and over again. One solution is to have a lot of animation and behaviors to pick from, but this can be expensive from both an authoring and memory standpoint. The ideas presented in this section can help to create the illusion of variation without requiring prohibitively large amounts of content.

4.6.1.1 Contextual One-Off Animations

Games generally make use of a large number of looping animations to communicate fundamental NPC actions such as idling or moving. While it's important to include variations of these animations, they tend to be longer in length compared to other animations in the game. If we were to create a lot of variation for each of these cycles, we would quickly run out of both development time and memory. Consider walking, for example. People within a similar context (the same height, age, and mental state) walk in a similar fashion. Either changes to this cycle will not be very noticeable or they will look unnatural. It is the smaller nonlooping actions and movements, such as changes in stride, shifts in weight, or looking around, that differentiate how one walks from another.

Contextual one-off animations add variety and help to break up looping animations. By matching the context of the looping animation, they further communicate a character's behavior to the player. These animations do not interrupt the underlying behavior, but instead desynchronize and vary them. Continuing with the example of walking, examples of some contextual one-offs might include stopping to scratch your leg, shifting your weight from side to side, and an animation to smoke (played as a mask on a different layer to save memory). These one-offs can be motion corrected to match both the current speed and the trajectory of the motion. For full-body one-offs, we use phase matching to transition seamlessly in and out of the one-off animation and back to the underlying looping animation. Most importantly, the contextual one-offs contain only the change we want to make to the base animation, so they are much smaller and can be reused across different contexts, which significantly increases the amount of variation we can create given a particular animation budget.

4.6.1.2 Micro Behaviors

Just as we can break up looping animations with smaller one-offs to create the illusion of variation within them, we can also extend this idea to vary behaviors themselves through the use of micro behaviors. Micro behaviors can be thought of as smaller subbehaviors that can run their logic in parallel with a core behavior, simply to provide variation. These behaviors can also temporarily interrupt a core behavior to perform a specific action, returning back to the core behavior after completion. Similar to animation one-offs, we can make use of a wide variety of micro behaviors to support the core behavior and break up behavior synchronization.

For example, imagine a combat situation with two NPCs that are executing a cover behavior. While in cover, they are peeking and shooting, evaluating for better cover, etc. One of the NPCs decides to reposition, and before the character performs this action, it shares this information with all other NPCs that are part of that scene. The cover behavior (i.e., being executed by all NPCs in cover) can include a micro behavior that reads this and plays a one-off animation to order an NPC to reposition. This doesn't need to be synchronized and runs independently on each NPC. The behavior logic chooses how often to select these micro behaviors. What's more, like contextual one-offs, micro behaviors can often be reused across multiple behaviors.

Another advantage to micro behaviors is that, in addition to creating variety, they can be used to clearly communicate the NPC's intent, making the reasoning behind the core behaviors apparent to the player. This is a crucial part of behavior variation. We often focus on tweaking values or adjusting utility formulae to make the NPC execute a behavior slightly differently. While this form of variation in behavior is important, if we don't clearly support this, it may be barely noticed by the player. Making the reasoning behind the behaviors obvious to the player allows the player to interact with them in meaningful ways. If the player doesn't understand what's happening, it might as well not be happening at all.

4.6.1.3 Using Additives with Idles

Idle animations suffer from the same issues described previously. They are cyclical and long. Additionally, they require a lot of variation to be compelling enough to notice. To deal with this problem, we can use a set of noise-based additive animations on a large number of idle poses (single-frame animations). These additive animations are played on a different animation layer and are unsynchronized with the base idle pose to add extra variation. This can create a large amount of variation from single-frame idle animations, which can save a great deal of animation memory and production time.

4.6.2 Behavior Distribution

One often overlooked aspect of NPC behaviors is how behaviors are distributed among a group of NPCs. NPCs whose behaviors are synchronized to happen at just the same time easily break the player's suspension of disbelief. In this section, we will look at ways to assign and distribute NPC behaviors.

4.6.2.1 Action Tokens

We often need to control how often a specific action occurs. For example, while a group of NPCs are executing their cover behavior, we might need to control how often an NPC throws a grenade. We can use the concept of action tokens to help with this. Each action that can be executed by multiple NPCs is assigned a particular number of tokens, and before an NPC can execute an action, they must acquire one of these tokens. For example, characters that want to shoot at the player when moving all can share a set of "move and shoot tokens." These tokens are used to limit the number of characters that can be moving and shooting at the same time.

The token system should support designer-specified parameters for each type of action. For example, the designers might want to specify the minimum amount of time that an NPC must wait after releasing a token before acquiring it again and whether the number of tokens should scale based on the number of characters in the scene. Using these sorts of parameters, we can control not only how often an action occurs but also how it is distributed across multiple characters.

4.6.2.2 Blackboards

In order to facilitate communication between logic that is spread across different behaviors for an individual character as well as among multiple characters, we can make use of data blackboards. These data blackboards can be defined at a global, group, or local level. All characters have access to the global blackboard, characters that are part of a specific context, have access to that context's group blackboard (e.g., all of the passengers in a vehicle might share a group blackboard), and finally each individual character always has access to its own local blackboard. Through the blackboards, we can communicate and manage actions and behaviors for the NPCs within a specific scene, while still keeping the logic independent of each other.

4.6.2.3 Action Ranking

In addition to action tokens, we can evaluate and assign a unique rank to each character within a specific situation. For example, all NPCs that are currently engaged in combat can be given a combat action rank. We can then assign specific actions or behaviors to characters with different ranks or rank categories.

These action ranks can be used to ensure that the NPCs that are most relevant to the player are the ones that execute the most interesting behavior. We can use a simple utility-based formula to determine the ranks. Factors such as the distance to the player, whether the character is visible to the player, whether the player is aiming at the character, and event-based values such as hearing gunfire or receiving damage from a bullet can be used to calculate the action rank. The event-based stimuli can be limited to influence the action rank for a set period of time (which should be specified by the designer).

Some behaviors can be scripted to execute unique rank-specific micro behaviors to further add variation within the scene. For example, a character holding a high action rank may be allowed to taunt the player. In addition, we can use ranks to specify unique behaviors for particular characters before allowing their systemic AI to run. For example, we can require high-action-ranked NPCs to stand and shoot the player for a few seconds, when the player first initiates combat with a particular group of NPCs. This gives the player a few targets to engage with first, while the others scatter for cover, rather than just allowing everyone to rush for cover.

4.6.2.4 On-Screen Realization

In order to make our behaviors more player centric, we can distribute behaviors based on what the player is actually seeing. For example, we can use on-screen realization as part of our utility ranking to ensure that NPCs that are on-screen receive a higher action ranking than those offscreen. We can also use on-screen realization to influence behavior execution. For example, we can ensure that NPCs that are on-screen choose cover or goal positions that do not cause them to run offscreen (which is often annoying to the player).

4.7 Conclusion

AI character development must include a strong focus on the synergy between animation and behavior. Having the right mindset and focus on realizing characters ensures that our NPCs make appropriate and intended decisions while still maintaining a strong sense of believability. This effort contributes significantly to the overall player experience.

Using animation techniques that focus on creating coverage while preserving the original authored animations, using a minimal amount of content, and reusing animation content, we can strive to maintain a high level of overall fidelity while keeping our memory budget in check. When it comes to motion, our emphasis is on displaying behavioral intent, variation, and preservation of momentum.

Finally, it is important to focus on solutions that explicitly manage variety and that distribute behaviors between characters. This level of realization control, centered on the player, guarantees a consistently positive experience.

5

Using Queues to Model a Merchant's Inventory

John Manslow

5.1 Introduction

Queues frequently appear in game worlds. Sometimes they are obvious—like the queues formed by cars in a traffic jam or patients waiting to see a doctor. At other times, they are more difficult to identify—like the queues formed by items in the inventory of a merchant. M/M/1 queues arise when objects are added to, and removed from, a collection at random time intervals and can be used to model such processes even when the order of the objects is not important.

This chapter will describe how to use the statistical properties of M/M/1 queues to efficiently simulate how they change over time. To provide a practical example, the chapter will show how to represent the inventory of a merchant as a set of M/M/1 queues and demonstrate how to efficiently generate realistic and mutually consistent random realizations of the inventory that take account of the levels of supply and demand. The book's website (http://www.gameaipro.com) includes a full implementation of everything that is described in the article.

5.2 M/M/1 Queues

An M/M/1 queue is a process in which objects are added to, and removed from, a collection at random intervals. The name M/M/1 is actually a form of Kendall's notation [Zabinsky 13], which is used to classify queues and indicates that additions and removals are memoryless (the time of one addition or removal does not affect the time of another) and that the queue consists of only a single collection. The random timings of the additions and removals mean that the number of objects in the collection—the length of the queue—changes randomly with time. Although this makes it impossible to predict the length of the queue with any certainty, it is possible to model it using two probability distributions, the stationary distribution and the transient distribution.

The stationary distribution models the length of queue that one would expect to see if the queuing process had been running for a very long time before it was observed. It is therefore useful for describing the length of a queue when it is encountered by the player for the first time. If objects are added to a queue at an average rate of add_rate per unit time and removed from it at an average rate of $remove\_rate$ per unit time, then its stationary distribution is

$$p(n) = \left(1 - rate\_ratio\right) \cdot rate\_ratio^n \tag{5.1}$$

where

$$rate\_ratio = \frac{add\_rate}{remove\_rate} \tag{5.2}$$

and $p(n)$ is the probability of the length of the queue being n items.

Note that, for a queue to be of finite length, it is necessary for $rate\_ratio$ to be strictly less than one. In other words, if the merchant's inventory isn't going to grow without bound, things need to be leaving the store faster than they are coming in. In general, the average length of an M/M/1 queue is $1/(1 - rate\_ratio)$, and the probability of observing an empty queue is $1 - rate\_ratio$.

Players naturally expect to encounter queues of specific lengths and not strange quantum queues in weird superpositions of states. It is therefore necessary to create a specific realization of a queue when the player first observes it by sampling from its stationary distribution. A simple way to do that is to generate a random number x that is greater than or equal to zero and less than one and, starting at $n = 0$, add the values of $p(n)$ until their sum exceeds x and then take n to be the length of the queue. This approach is implemented in `MM1Queue::GetSample`.

The transient distribution describes the length of a queue that has already been observed and is therefore useful when a player encounters a queue for anything other than the first time. If, t units of time ago, the player observed a queue to be of length m, its transient distribution is [Baccelli 89]

$$p(n \,|\, t, m) = e^{-(add\_rate + remove\_rate) \cdot t} \cdot \left[p_1 + p_2 + p_3 \right] \tag{5.3}$$

where

$$p_1 = rate\_ratio^{\frac{n-m}{2}} \cdot I_{n-m}(at)$$ (5.4)

$$p_2 = rate\_ratio^{\frac{n-m-1}{2}} \cdot I_{n+m+1}(at)$$ (5.5)

$$p_3 = (1 - rate\_ratio) \cdot rate\_ratio^n \sum_{j=n+m+2}^{\infty} rate\_ratio^{-\frac{j}{2}} \cdot I_{n+m+1}(at)$$ (5.6)

and

$$a = 2 \times remove\_rate\sqrt{rate\_ratio},$$ (5.7)

$I_n(\cdot)$ is the modified Bessel function of the first kind, which is computed by MathUtilities::Iax, and $p(n\,|\,t,m)$ is the probability that the length of the queue is n, which is computed by MM1Queue::GetStateProbability. Once again, it is necessary to create a specific realization of the queue, and that can be done using the procedure that has already been described, but substituting $p(n\,|\,t,m)$ for $p(n)$. This approach is implemented in the overload of MM1Queue::GetSample that takes time and count parameters.

Because both the stationary and transient distributions are derived from a statistical model of the queuing process, samples that are drawn from them naturally satisfy all common sense expectations as to how queues change over time. In particular,

- Queues with high rates of addition and low rates of removal will usually be long
- Queues with low rates of addition and high rates of removal will usually be short
- The effects of player interactions will disappear with time—slowly for queues with low rates of addition and removal and quickly for queues with high rates of addition and removal
- Queues will change little if the time between observations is short, especially for queues with low rates of addition and removal
- Queues will change a lot if the time between observations is long, especially for queues with high rates of addition and removal

The first row of Table 5.1 gives the stationary distribution for a queue with $add\_rate = 0.5$ (one addition every other unit of time on average) and $remove\_rate = 1.0$ (one removal per unit of time on average). Assuming that the player observes the queue to be of length two at time zero and adds four objects to it, the following rows show the transient distribution 0.01, 0.1, 1, 10, and 100 units of time later. It is important to note that these rows show how the transient distribution would evolve if the queue remained unobserved and hence no concrete realizations were produced. For example, 10 units of time after the player had observed the queue, there would be a 0.103 probability of the queue being 3 objects long.

Table 5.1 An Example of an Equilibrium Distribution and Transient Distributions

Time, t	Queue Length, n								
	0	1	2	3	4	5	6	7	8
0.00	0.500	0.250	0.125	0.063	0.031	0.016	0.008	0.004	0.002
0.01	0.000	0.000	0.000	0.000	0.000	0.010	0.985	0.005	0.000
0.10	0.000	0.000	0.000	0.000	0.004	0.087	0.865	0.043	0.001
1.00	0.000	0.002	0.010	0.042	0.131	0.284	0.349	0.142	0.033
10.00	0.315	0.186	0.131	0.103	0.082	0.063	0.046	0.031	0.020
100.00	0.500	0.250	0.125	0.063	0.031	0.016	0.008	0.004	0.002

The transient distribution makes it possible to model how the length of a queue changes after it has been observed but provides no way of determining how many of the individual objects that were originally in the queue are still there when it is observed again. That kind of information is useful when the objects are uniquely identifiable. For example, cars parked on a street will have different colors and be different makes and models, and people waiting in a hospital will have different clothing and facial features.

If the objects are processed on a strictly first-come, first-served basis, then the number that remain in the queue from the previous observation can roughly be estimated by taking the original length of the queue and subtracting a sample from a Poisson distribution that represents the number of objects processed since the queue was last observed.

If the objects are processed in a random order, the number that remain can be approximated by taking a sample from the same Poisson distribution and then using it in conjunction with a binomial distribution to estimate the number of objects in the original queue that were processed. Technically, this is equivalent to assuming that the length of the queue remained the same between the two observations, but it produces realistic-looking estimates even when that is not actually the case. Implementations of both techniques can be found in the `Inventory::GenerateRealization` overload that takes the time parameter.

Before finishing the discussion of M/M/1 queues, it is important to highlight the fact that the expressions for the stationary and transient distributions assume that the average rates at which objects are added to, and removed from, the queue are constant. This assumption holds for many natural processes but breaks down when additions or removals occur in bursts. Such bursts will occur in relation to the numbers of cars waiting at an intersection, for example, due to the presence of a neighboring intersection or the effects of traffic signals. In such cases, the theoretical deficiencies of M/M/1 queues will often not be apparent to the player and can be ignored, but, in some cases, it will be necessary to use an alternative model [Zabinsky 13].

This section has described the basic properties of M/M/1 queues, given expressions for the stationary and transient distributions of queue length, and shown how to sample from those distributions to generate consistent realizations when queues are encountered by the player. The following section will describe how M/M/1 queues can be used to model the inventory of a merchant to produce random inventories that are consistent with each other, with the levels of supply and demand of each type of item in the inventory and with the player's observations and interactions with the merchant.

5.3 Modeling a Merchant's Inventory

In a large, open world game with dozens of merchants, hundreds of NPCs, and tens of thousands of individual inventory items, it is impractical to explicitly model economic activity in real time in enough detail to track the inventory of each merchant. Fortunately, to make the world believable, it is sufficient to generate random inventories each time a merchant is encountered provided that they are consistent with players' common sense expectations as to how they should change with time.

In terms of the numbers of each type of item in an inventory, those expectations are essentially the same as those for the lengths of queues that were given earlier. This strongly suggests that a merchant's inventory can be modeled in the following way:

1. Create one M/M/1 queue for each type of item the merchant can have in his or her inventory.
2. Set the average rate at which each type of item is added to its queue to be equal to the average rate at which the merchant will buy it.
3. Set the average rate at which each type of item is removed from its queue to be equal to the average rate at which the merchant will sell it when he or she has it.
4. When the player first encounters the merchant, create his or her inventory by sampling from the stationary distribution for each type of item.
5. On all subsequent encounters, create his or her inventory by sampling from the transient distribution for each type of item.

Even though real merchants do not buy and sell at random, steps 2 and 3 ensure that the merchant's inventory is generally consistent with the levels of supply and demand for each type of item, and step 5 ensures that players see an inventory that is consistent from one visit to the next.

Table 5.2 gives an example of how the numbers of three inventory items—truffles, arrows, and swords—vary with time, which, in this example, is measured in game world hours. Truffles are assumed to have limited supply (only one is added to the inventory every 1000 h on average) but high demand (one is sold every hour on average), arrows are assumed to have high supply (one is added every hour on average) and high demand (one is sold every 0.98 h on average), and swords are assumed to have low supply (one is added every 200 h on average) and low demand (one is sold every 100 h on average).

Table 5.2 An Example of How a Simple Three-Item Inventory Changes with Time

	Item		
Time (h)	Truffles	Arrows	Swords
0	0	83	1
0 after player interaction	5	33	1
1	3	33	1
48	0	37	1
100	0	26	0
200	0	47	0

The numbers of truffles, arrows, and swords at time zero—when the player encounters the merchant for the first time—are obtained by sampling from each type of item's stationary distribution. The player sells the merchant five truffles and buys 50 arrows and then explores the environment for 1 h. He or she then returns to the merchant, and a new inventory is generated by sampling from each type of item's transient distribution. This reveals that the merchant still has three truffles left and the number of arrows and swords hasn't changed. Returning to the merchant after 48 h reveals that all truffles have been sold and the merchant has 37 arrows. The code that was used to generate the numbers in this example is included on the book's website.

The basic inventory model that has been described so far can easily be enhanced to simulate more complex behavior. For example, a merchant might buy 50 arrows every Monday but only if he has fewer than 50 arrows in stock. This kind of behavior can be closely approximated by sampling from the distribution for the number of arrows in the merchant's inventory from the previous Monday and adding 50 if the sample is less than 50. The resulting number can then be used as a "virtual observation" when sampling from the current transient distribution to obtain the current number of arrows—the game simply behaves as though the player had been present the previous Monday and seen how many arrows the merchant had.

Similar logic can be used if the merchant always buys enough arrows to bring his or her stock up to 50, if the arrow vendor comes randomly rather than every Monday, or if the supply of arrows is not entirely dependable. The merchant buying additional stock is only one type of special event that affects the numbers of items in his inventory. Another might be the death of a nobleman, causing the merchant to suddenly acquire a large number of luxury items at the resulting estate sale or the commander of a local garrison buying up all of the armor. Such events can be modeled in a similar way to the merchant's buying behavior; a virtual observation of the affected inventory item can be created for the time of the event and used in the transient distribution when the player encounters the merchant.

Other events might cause permanent changes in the levels of supply and demand, and they can be simulated by changing *add_rate* and *remove_rate*. For example, a new mine might open up, leading to an increase in the supply of iron. This effect can be simulated by making a virtual observation of the amount of iron that the merchant had in stock when the mine opened by sampling from a distribution with the old values of *add_rate* and *remove_rate*. That observation would then be used in the transient distribution with the new values of *add_rate* and *remove_rate* when the player encountered the merchant. If the levels of supply and demand change multiple times between encounters, the effects of the changes can be simulated by multiple virtual observations that are obtained using the previous observation, the previous values of *add_rate* and *remove_rate*, and the sampling from the transient distribution. The game would thus behave as though the player had observed the level of stock of the affected type of item each time its supply and demand changed.

In some cases, it is desirable to ensure that a merchant always has a certain minimum number of items of a particular type in stock. If a game directs the player to travel a long way to buy special items, for example, it would be very frustrating to arrive at the destination only to discover that the items were not available. This problem can easily be solved by adding a constant to the number of items generated by the stationary distribution on the player's first encounter. If the merchant should generally maintain a certain minimum stock level, then adding a constant is unsatisfactory because it does not adequately model the dynamics of how stock changes in response to interactions with the player—if the player buys all the stock, for example, the amount of stock needs to recover in a convincing way.

The simplest solution to this problem is to model the merchant regularly buying new stock, as was described earlier. Alternately, it is possible to create a reserve of items that can only be purchased by the player and model how it recovers over time if the player makes a purchase that depletes it. This is done by estimating the number of items that could have been added to the reserve since it was depleted if the merchant repopulated it by buying items at a rate of *add_rate* and selling nothing. If the reserve could only have been partially repopulated, the reserve is the full extent of the inventory, and no sample from the transient distribution is required. If the reserve could have been fully repopulated, however, the time when the process of repopulation would've been completed is calculated, and the number of nonreserve items is obtained by sampling from the transient distribution using a virtual observation of zero nonreserve items backdated to when the reserve would've reached full strength. This technique is implemented in the overload of `Inventory::GenerateRealization` that takes the time parameter.

Finally, some types of items, such as arrows, are naturally traded in batches, and it is unlikely that a merchant would buy or sell only a single instance of such types. This effect can be approximated by using stationary and transient distributions to represent the numbers of batches held by the merchant rather than the numbers of individual items. When the number of batches changes from the player's last observation, the number of items can be generated randomly by assuming that a particular number of batches would correspond to a particular range of numbers of items. For example, if each batch of arrows is of size 25, then one batch would correspond to between 1 and 25 arrows, two batches, 26 and 50 arrows, etc. If a sample from the distribution specified a stock level of two batches, the actual number of items would be chosen randomly from the range 26 to 50.

In general, the properties of M/M/1 queues that were described earlier make it possible to guess values for parameters like *add_rate* and *remove_rate* to simulate specific behaviors. It is, however, important to validate those behaviors using a simple test application like the one included on the book's website that allows the behaviors to be quickly and efficiently evaluated over a wide range of timescales.

5.3.1 Computational Considerations

A game might contain many thousands of different types of items that could potentially be found in an inventory, so the question naturally arises as to whether it's computationally practical to sample from such a large number of queues. Fortunately, for types where *rate_ratio* is small (i.e., for types that are unlikely to appear in the inventory or to only be present in small numbers—such as truffles and swords), samples can be obtained at a rate of hundreds of thousands per second per core on a typical desktop PC. Where *rate_ratio* is close to one—as was the case with the arrows—samples can only be obtained at a rate of thousands per second, so the approach described in this chapter might not be suitable for inventories where hundreds of different types of items are likely to be present in hundreds or thousands. Such inventories are likely to be the exception, however, and it is important to remember that samples are only required when a player encounters a merchant—there's no ongoing computation—and that samples for each type of item are independent, and hence the process of sampling can, if necessary, easily be distributed across multiple cores and multiple frames.

5.4 Conclusion

This article has described M/M/1 queues and showed how they can be simulated in a consistent and computationally efficient way by sampling from their stationary and transient distributions. It has shown how they can be used to represent the inventory of a merchant in such a way that it remains consistent with each item's supply and demand, the player's observations of the inventory, and the player's interactions with the merchant. This provides a simple and efficient way to simulate how the inventory of a merchant changes with time.

References

[Baccelli 89] Baccelli, F., Massey, W. A. 1989. A sample path analysis of the M/M/1 queue. *Journal of Applied Probability*, 26(2): 418–422. https://www.princeton.edu/~wmassey/20th%20Century/sample%20path%20MM1.pdf (accessed July 20, 2014).

[Zabinsky 13] Zabinsky, Z. 2013. Stochastic models and decision analysis, University of Washington, Seattle, WA. http://courses.washington.edu/inde411/QueueingTheory.pdf (accessed July 20, 2014).

Psychologically Plausible Methods for Character Behavior Design

Phil Carlisle

6.1 Introduction

If you have ever worked with 3D game character artists, you'll have heard them talk obsessively about silhouette and how a character reads. They do this because they understand that for video games especially, there is the issue of viewpoint. As players move around a world in 3D, they can change their viewpoint with respect to the character considerably, changing distance and angle. Artists want their work to be understood by players, so they try and maximize that understanding by taking care to make a "readable" character. A readable character is one that can be viewed from different directions and at different distances and still remain recognizable.

As behavior designers, we have very similar issues to deal with; we have to make our behaviors "readable" by players in different situations and have our players recognize and understand the behavior. The aim of this chapter is to encourage you to think about this aspect of your behavior design and to ground you in a sample of the psychological aspects that come into play from the player's perspective. Using a number of studies performed by groups of undergraduate game design students as examples, the intention is to raise awareness rather than to be academically rigorous. As psychology is a very complex field, it is recommended that these studies not be taken at face value, but instead should be used to consider how psychology might inform the development of character behavior, by adding methods of evaluation and ways of thinking about player understanding.

6.2 Perception and Abstractions

When working on character behaviors, one of the principal tools at our disposal is the use of animation and movement. By the use of movement, we can convey to the player different behavioral meanings based on the nature of the movement, but how do players actually perceive movement?

In the 1970s, psychologist Gunnar Johansson ran a series of studies involving point-light animations [Johansson 73]. He took a number of his students and dressed them completely in black clothing. He then attached small reflective markers to various joints and got the students to act out particular motions while filming them such that only the markers were visible. The resulting films bear a striking resemblance to modern motion-capture data; an example of his work can be viewed online [Maas 11].

Johansson was interested in our perception of motion. What he found was that from these relatively sparse data, his test subjects were able to describe what types of objects were involved and in some circumstances what gender the subject was. He varied the angles of the motions and otherwise manipulated the viewpoints in order to study where perception broke down. Interestingly, when he tested occluding some of the markers, the participants were able to perceive the motion until a relatively high percentage of the markers were obscured. Similarly, he altered the orientation and found that perception broke down only in fairly extreme circumstances (e.g., when the subject was turned upside down).

What this perception study showed is that humans (and presumably other animals) have a capability to take relatively sparse or abstract motions and parse them into familiar mental models of motion. We can think of this process as *shape fitting*, taking motion, and mapping it to known patterns of movement and then attributing that movement to some previously learned behavior.

It seems likely that this capability is actually a very useful one in terms of neuroevolution; for instance, it might be used to spot a prey animal from a distance by its movement pattern or for selecting a weaker prey animal from a herd.

So what does this all have to do with character AI? The basic premise proposed here is that when we create behavior, we should take care that the motion the behavior exhibits matches motions that can then be shape fitted by players into mental models that allow them to associate the motion of the character with learned patterns.

Just to highlight this point, consider a character behavior in the abstract for a moment. If we want to portray an aggressive character, what styles of movement would we most likely select to show that aggression? One suggestion would be that short, fast movements would be better for showing aggression than long, slow movements. Why would this be the case? One possibility is that we have evolved a capability to detect sharp fast movements as aggressive in response to the types of movements we might have seen from predator animals. For example, think of a cat trying to attack a mouse; how does the movement change as the cat approaches? Think of the explosive force used for when the cat "pounces" on the mouse.

6. Psychologically Plausible Methods for Character Behavior Design

This sharp fast movement happens in other animals too. Fish, insects, and snakes all exhibit striking motions. Most 3D animators know this instinctively, but this notion of movement speed was actually outlined much earlier in traditional stop-motion animation as the principle of force described well in *The Illusion of Life* [Thomas 81] and essentially deals with the biomechanical effort involved in specific motions. The act of stalking in the cat movement might be seen as aggressive by a viewer who had previously seen the cat hunting. From the perspective of the prey, however, the slower movement is less threatening, which suggests that viewpoint has a large impact on the way movement is perceived and is informed by the previous experience of the viewer.

Another interesting aspect to come out of Johansson's work is the fact that some motions suggest particular feelings or relationships. In one study, the motions of two point lights were arranged such that a synchronized circular motion was used, as shown in Figure 6.1. Where the point lights gained close proximity and mirrored the motion of each other, this was perceived by viewers as having affinity between the points. Similarly, points that moved in contrary motions were perceived to have animosity.

In order to cement this notion of perception of motion in the abstract, let us present another study that will also ease us into another aspect of psychology.

In 1944, Fritz Heider and Marianne Simmel presented a paper called *An Experimental Study of Apparent Behavior* [Heider 44]. In it, they describe a study where they presented viewers with a film showing a number of abstract shapes (lines, circles, triangles) with corresponding motions filmed using stop-motion animation. They asked the participants to explain what they saw in the film. In almost all of the cases, the participants explained the film in terms of what the "characters" were doing. They described the scene with explanations such as the following: "A man has planned to meet a girl and the girl comes along

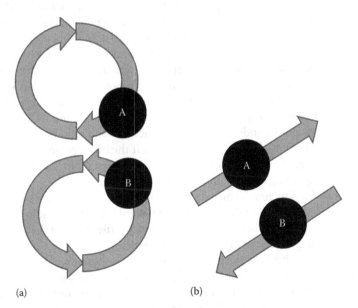

(a)　　　　　　　　(b)

Figure 6.1

An example of complementary (a) and contrary (b) motions used in the study.

with another man. The first man tells the second to go; the second tells the first, and he shakes his head. Then the two men have a fight, and the girl starts to go into the room to get out of the way and hesitates and finally goes in," clearly showing that they had generated an internal narrative to explain what they saw. Indeed it is hard not to see the same footage [Smith-Welch 08] and offer a similar explanation.

The fact that viewers of a film are able to take abstract shapes with motion and construct an internal narrative should really drive home the point that we need to consider the qualities of motion inherent in behavior when we are trying to design characters. Once again, this points to the ability to map relatively abstract movements to known behavioral patterns. As character designers, this should give us some ideas on how to shape the understanding of a character's behavior from a player's perspective. Altering the qualities of movement and the viewpoint they are seen from could allow us to alter how a character is perceived to our advantage, much like an author setting up a reader's mental view of a character before getting them to perform an action.

6.3 Developmental Psychology and the Teleological Stance

The process by which we are able to translate movements into mental models and the specifics of that process is an ongoing area of research. The term "shape fitting" relates it to the processes used in computer vision, but this is merely a shorthand description for a complex set of processes. It is quite useful to review this aspect within the literature on developmental psychology. A useful starting point is the *Blackwell Handbook of Childhood Cognitive Development* [Goshwani 10]. In particular, the chapter by Gergely [Gergely 10] describes an early infant process that allows inference about actions through a naive theory of rational action, basically a process of mapping movements to intended actions that is referred to as the teleological stance. As infants grow, they develop more capabilities in terms of the ability to read a given motion and infer its intention, so developers of games for infants should probably consider the stages of development their target audience has reached.

This ability to read the intentions of others uses gaze direction as a key component. Children follow the gaze direction of their parents in order to learn what is important for them to be aware of [Goshwani 10]. Over time, they develop the capacity to model the knowledge of others, using gaze as a significant aspect of that model. For example, as a child grows, they begin to understand that another person might have knowledge of a particular object or they might not. They learn that if the other person has actually seen the object (i.e., directed their gaze toward it), then they know about the object. Thus, they learn that the stronger the gaze, the more important the object.

This aspect of gaze direction is important for us as behavior designers because it is one of the primary tools we can use to direct the player toward the correct reading of behavioral intent. The player can read the behavior quite differently if they see that the character is not aware of an interacting object; in other words, if we direct the gaze of the character away from an object, we can alter how the player reads any corresponding interaction with it.

Consider Figure 6.2 as an example. In the leftmost pair, we have no way of determining the gaze direction. If you focus on that pair exclusively, you are unlikely to ascribe any intention to the objects. In the middle pair, the gaze is pointing inward; this is likely to indicate antagonism or aggression, unless we have previously seen context in which the pair had displayed positive affect, in which case we might view them as being in a friendly

Figure 6.2

A simple example of how perceived gaze direction can influence our reading of a situation.

chat or a conspiratorial congress. The final pair we might well view as being unaware of each other, unless we had seen previous context that suggested they knew each other, might then change the reading of the pair to one of a social rebuff. However, if you interpret the "characters" in the figure, you should be aware that the only condition that is changing is the perceived gaze direction of each pair. This effect is happening even within a very abstract scene but can be particularly strong when seen in motion.

6.4 Attribution Theory

The work by Heider, Simmel, and others eventually led to the field of psychology known as attribution theory [Kelley 67]. For behavior design, this concept of *attribution* is an important one. The basic idea is to consider how we attribute the intention of an action. We commonly think of actions as internal (i.e., the character intended to do it) or external (it was done to the character or caused by other factors). As behavior designers, we should be able to influence a player's view of the behavior such that they ascribe the action as being intentional by the character or unintentionally happening to the character. For instance, we might hint at the incompetence of a character, which leads the player to likely ascribe positive actions as being external; in other words, if something good happens, it happens by chance and not skill.

An interesting aspect of the Heider/Simmel study was that the narrative given to explain the scene changed when the scene was presented in reverse; each viewer was presented with both a "forward" normal viewing of the film and a "reverse" viewing, in which the film was played backward. In many areas, the narrative broke down because the context of the motions was changed. For instance, the larger triangle in the forward presentation is seen as dominant or bullying through the remaining narrative due to an early segment where it performs a fast motion toward the smaller triangle and pushes it a short distance; however, in the reverse presentation, the first aggressive "push" movement is not seen, and thus the narrative of dominance is changed. This implies that in order for a viewer to correctly attribute a behavior, that behavior must be seen within a context that is temporally plausible; in other words, the order in which we present behavioral movements is important. It can be useful to recreate this aspect of the study with your own section of a film, playing the film in the reverse and thinking about how the behaviors are affected. Are some behaviors still understandable? Do you read the motivations of characters differently? What is causing that effect?

We can consider a simple illustration of this effect. Think of a cat trying to catch a mouse; imagine the cat slowly creeping up behind the mouse, keeping close to the ground, slowly moving up, and then suddenly moving with rapid force during a "pounce" behavior.

Now consider the behavior with the order of actions reversed. Instead of a creep-then-pounce, think how a pounce-then-creep would look.

The concept of attribution of behavior is an interesting one, in that it poses questions about awareness and intent. If we are constantly evaluating the motions of others in a bid to understand their intention in terms of our own beliefs about them, then perhaps we can start to manipulate that evaluation in order to achieve a desired effect. One of the key aspects we need to think about is the attribution of intent. Does a behavior we want to portray show intention for the character or not? For example, imagine two characters and a ball. Character A throws the ball at character B; only character B is facing away from A and is not aware of the ball, so consequently B gets hit on the head. In this simple scene, we can actually influence different readings of the inference of the viewer.

Consider the case where we have previously shown character A throwing balls at other characters. In this case, it is likely a viewer would ascribe the ball-throwing behavior as an intentional act. The viewer will have learned that character A throws balls and thus would see the ball-throwing action as fitting in with what they know about A's likelihood to intentionally throw a ball at another character.

Now imagine the same scene, but instead we have previously seen character B being hit by several other characters throwing balls. In this case, we are more likely to attribute the behavior to be a lack of awareness by B than any particular malice by character A.

The fact that a simple ball-throwing behavior could be understood differently depending on our understanding of the attributed qualities of the participants is an important point to note in any character behavior design. We can begin to manipulate a player's reading of a given character by reinforcing their mental attribution processes if we can set up scenes in a manner that takes into account the teleological stance of the behavior and reinforces a given view of the character.

6.5 Problem of Characters as Tokens

Before we get on to discussing the practical application of these psychological principles in terms of behavior design, it is worth noting an issue that most character designers face. A number of years ago at the University of Bolton, we ran an (unpublished) undergraduate study into the methods that players use to select companion characters in games. In this particular study, the test involved choosing companion characters for further gameplay from a roster of characters, which were presented in different ways. The characters themselves were portrayed using different clothing and gender options, with the aim of the study being to understand more about the effect of the communication mode (text, cinematic) on the choice. One of the more surprising results from the study came from the qualitative interviews conducted with participants after they had made the character choice. Although this was not the aim of the study, we found that most players chose characters not based on their narrative delivery method, but instead on a measure of perceived usefulness in the game. In essence, they had ignored the "character" of the choice and had instead chosen based on the utility value. This was not a choice that was based on evidence (no statistics were provided for comparing the characters) but rather on a simple perceived value, that is, "they looked like they would be good in a fight."

The fact that players understand that characters in games are also part of the game mechanics suggests an underlying problem in terms of making more believable characters,

6. Psychologically Plausible Methods for Character Behavior Design

in that for all our best efforts, we may never be able to break that relationship in the player's mind. It might well be that games with more focus on the story and setting of the game could convince players to choose characters for their narrative value; however, it is worth considering what aspects of a character players are likely to base their choices on at the design stage. Is the player presented with information on the character that will explicitly state their utility? How can we identify players who make choices based on other aspects of character and perhaps alter our offering of choices based on that identification?

6.6 Practical Application of Psychology in Character Behavior Design

In another study, an undergraduate group was interested in how the perception of a character shaped a player's view of their own performance. They conducted an experiment in which test subjects played an online game against a series of three "bots" where each bot was represented with a different narrative designed to relate to easy, medium, and hard opponent difficulty levels. What the test subjects were not aware of was that each of the three "bots" was actually being controlled by a human player, who was deliberately playing to a script that essentially reduced the combat to the same level of difficulty for each play session. What the study found was that the players were more likely to score their own performance highly if they managed to win against the "hard" enemy. Similarly, they sought to attribute a loss to the difficulty level of the opponent. This study essentially showed that players can be influenced to feel differently about their own performance depending on the narrative context of their actions. If the context is one where the player feels they are likely to lose, then they ascribe a loss to the game, whereas if they win they are more likely to ascribe the win to their own mastery or skill, no matter of the actual difficulty involved in the action.

In practical terms, this means we can start to encourage players to feel more skillful by presenting them with challenges described as hard, but which are biased toward them winning. This can be as subtle as describing enemies in a manner that inflates their ability with respect to other agents, for example, calling an agent a major instead of a soldier. We can also influence a player's perception by making sure they see a character fail at a task; from that point, it is more likely they will perceive that character as more likely to fail other tasks.

Similarly, we can influence a player's perception of character interactions within a group by carefully manipulating their motions. Considering the case where a player is controlling a group of role-playing characters, we can make two characters within that group appear more friendly toward each other by simply biasing their movements to be more complementary (i.e., often aligned in the same direction, being in close proximity). We can increase the perception of animosity by making sure that the characters avoid close proximity and bias their movements such that they never mirror each other.

6.7 Conclusion

When designing the behaviors of characters in a game, it can be too easy to focus on the individual behavior and lose sight of the overall readability of the character. If we want to create characters that players understand and believe in, we must embrace the aspects of psychology that inform how a player perceives them.

In this chapter, we have tried to offer some simple psychological theories that you can investigate and use to your advantage when considering your initial character designs. Hopefully, this chapter has convinced you that many of the psychological tools you can use to affect players' perceptions function at a high level of abstraction and can often be implemented with very minimal development cost.

Psychology itself is an ongoing area of research and we are only just beginning to investigate the psychology involved in games. From a practical point of view, many of the psychological effects described in this chapter are quite subtle or do not apply universally to all player types. Even with these caveats, it is well worth the time for a designer to familiarize themselves with psychology and its measurement as part of the design toolset. We have seen many of our students gain design roles within the game industry due in large part to their experience working on an aspect of game psychology that is under researched, offering a unique experience and perspective that many employers seem to find valuable.

References

[Gergely 10] Gergely, G. 2010. Kinds of agents: The origins of understanding instrumental and communicative agency. In *Blackwell Handbook of Childhood Cognitive Development* (2nd edn.), ed. U. Goshwani, pp. 76–105. Oxford, U.K.: Blackwell.

[Goshwani 10] Goshwani, U. ed. 2010. *Blackwell Handbook of Childhood Cognitive Development* (2nd edn.). Oxford, U.K.: Blackwell Publishers.

[Heider 44] Heider, F. and Simmel, M. 1944. An experimental study of apparent behavior. *The American Journal of Psychology* (University of Illinois Press) 57(2): 243–259.

[Johansson 73] Johansson, G. 1973. Visual perception of biological motion and a model for its analysis. *Perception and Psychophysics* (Springer-Verlag) 14(2): 201–211.

[Kelley 67] Kelley, H. H. 1967. Attribution theory in social psychology. *Nebraska Symposium on Motivation* (University of Nebraska Press) 15: 192–238.

[Maas 11] Maas, J. 2011. Johansson: Motion perception. https://www.youtube.com/watch?v=1F5ICP9SYLU (accessed June 1, 2014).

[Smith-Welch 08] Smith-Welch, M. Youtube.com. https://www.youtube.com/watch?v=sZBKer6PMtM (accessed June 2, 2014).

[Thomas 81] Thomas, F. and Johnson, O. 1981. *The Illusion of Life: Disney Animation.* New York: Hyperion.

7

Behavior Decision System
Dragon Age Inquisition's *Utility Scoring Architecture*

Sebastian Hanlon and Cody Watts

7.1 Introduction

The real-time combat sequences of *Dragon Age: Inquisition* (*DA:I*) pit the player-controlled Inquisitor in a fight to the death against shambling undead, fearsome demons, and—of course—towering dragons. It is a tough job, but the Inquisitor is not alone; fighting alongside his or her are three AI-controlled allies—fellow members of the Inquisition such as The Iron Bull, a towering, axe-swinging mercenary, Varric Tethras, a smooth-talking dwarf, and Dorian Pavus, a charming and quick-witted mage.

In *Dragon Age*, combat is driven by "abilities." A typical combatant will have anywhere from 2 to 20 abilities at their disposal, ranging from the simple ("hit your foe with the weapon you are holding") to the elaborate ("call down a rain of fire upon your enemies"). Each ability has an associated cost expressed in terms of a depletable resource called "mana" or "stamina." Because mana/stamina is limited, abilities also have an implicit opportunity cost—the mana/stamina consumed by one ability will inevitably preclude the use of future abilities. This creates a challenging problem for human players and AI characters

73

alike: When faced with limited resources, a plurality of choices, and a constantly changing game state, how can a combatant quickly identify the course of action which will yield the greatest possible benefit? For *DA:I*, we created a utility-based AI system called the Behavior Decision System (BDS) to answer this question and to handle the complex decision-making which combatants must perform. In this chapter, we will describe the principles and architecture of the BDS, providing you with the necessary information to implement a similar system and extend it to meet the needs of your own game.

7.2 The Behavior Decision System

The architecture of the BDS is based upon the following assumptions:

1. At any given time, there is a finite set of actions which an AI character can perform.
2. An AI character can only perform one action at a time.
3. Actions have differing utility values; some actions are more useful than others.
4. It is possible to quantify the utility of every action.

When taken together, these assumptions naturally suggest a simple greedy algorithm to determine an AI character's best course of action: Start by identifying the set of actions which it can legally take. Then, evaluate each action and assign it a score based on its utility. After each action has been evaluated, the action with the highest score is the action which should be taken (Graham 2014).

There are two major challenges to this approach. First, how can an AI character enumerate all the actions which it can perform? Second, how can an AI character qualify the utility of an action? Before an AI character can answer these questions, we must first impart it with knowledge—knowledge about itself and the world in which it lives.

Consider, for example, a simple action such as "drinking a health potion." Most human players know that it is useful to drink a health potion when their health is low. Unfortunately, AI characters do not intuitively understand concepts like life, death, health, and healing potions. They do not know that being alive is "good" and being dead is "bad." They do not understand that drinking a health potion at low health is good, but drinking a health potion at full health is wasteful. And they do not understand that health potions are consumable objects, and that one cannot drink a health potion unless one owns a health potion.

At its most basic level, the BDS is a framework which allows gameplay designers to impart knowledge to AI characters. Specifically, the BDS exists to provider answers to the following questions: Which actions can an AI character perform? Under what circumstances can they perform those actions? How should those actions be prioritized relative to each other? And finally: How can those actions actually be performed?

7.3 Enumerating Potential Actions

There are more than 60 abilities in *DA:I*, but many of these abilities can be used in different ways to achieve different purposes. For example the "Charging Bull" ability allows a warrior to charge directly into combat, damaging and knocking-aside any enemy who stands in his or her way. This is its intended, obvious purpose. However, this same ability can also be used as a way for an injured warrior to quickly retreat from combat. Though the underlying ability is the same, the motivation for the ability is completely different. Therefore, when enumerating potential actions, it is not sufficient to simply count the number of abilities at a character's disposal—we must also include the various ways in which those abilities can be performed. In order to distinguish between the various ways an ability can be used, we defined a data structure called a "behavior snippet."

Behavior snippets are the fundamental unit on which the BDS operates. Each snippet contains the information an AI character requires to evaluate and execute an ability in a particular way. In a sense, a snippet represents a fragment of knowledge—and throughout the game knowledge can be granted to characters by "registering" a snippet with to a character via the BDS. For example, a piece of weaponry may have one or more behavior snippets attached which tell AI characters how to use the weapon. When an AI character equips the weapon, these snippets will be registered to the character through the BDS. Similarly, when the weapon is unequipped, the snippets will be unregistered from that character.

Behavior snippets make it simple for the BDS to enumerate the list of actions available to a character; one merely needs to look at the set of registered snippets. The most complex AI characters in *DA:I* have over 50 behavior snippets registered simultaneously, though an average AI character will have 10–20 registered snippets.

7.4 Evaluating Behaviors

A behavior snippet contains the information an AI character requires to evaluate and execute an ability in a particular way—but what exactly does this mean? As stated previously, the BDS is based upon the assumption that it is possible to quantify the utility of every action. In order for this assumption to hold, each behavior snippet must contain within it a method to quantify the utility of the action it represents. There are many possible ways to quantify utility, but for *DA:I*, we chose to represent utility using a modified behavior tree which we call an "evaluation tree."

7.4.1 Calculating Utility

In the broadest possible terms, the purpose of an evaluation tree is simply to produce a score value for its associated behavior snippet. These scores can then be used as a basis for comparing two behavior snippets against each other in order to rank their relative utility. Score values are assigned via "scoring nodes" embedded within the evaluation tree itself. When the tree begins executing from its root node, it starts with a score of zero. As the tree progresses from one node to the next, any scoring nodes it executes will add their value to the tree's total score.

Evaluation trees are evaluated "in context"—that is to say, the nodes within the tree have access to information such as the AI character who is performing the evaluation. This allows for the creation of evaluation trees which produce different scores depending on the context in which they are evaluated (Merrill 2014). For example, Figure 7.1 shows an evaluation tree which will return a score of 5 if the evaluating character's health is less than 50%, and a score of 0 otherwise.

When constructing our scoring system, we considered various schemes for automatic normalization or scaling of scoring values. Ultimately, we chose to use (and recommend using) a designer-facing scoring convention to provide a framework for how actions

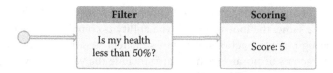

Figure 7.1

This evaluation tree returns different scores based on the health of the evaluating character.

Table 7.1 Scoring Framework Used in *Dragon Age: Inquisition*

Action Type	Point Values	Description
Basic	10	Preferable to doing nothing, and if multiple options are available, they are equivalent to each other.
Offensive	20–40	As a class, always preferable to basic actions, and compared against each other with 20 points of "urgency dynamic range" for prioritizing based on situational influences.
Support	25–45	As a class, preferable to offensive actions with the same level of "urgency," as they are either preparatory and should be used before engaging offensively, or used in reaction to emerging bad situations.
Reaction	50–70	All actions in this class have evaluation trees that respond to specific and immediate execution criteria (typically responding to an imminent threat to the AI character); if these criteria are present these actions should be executed in priority over any other (and otherwise valid) choices.

should be scored relative to each other. Note that these rules are guidance for content creators and have no explicit representation in game data. Table 7.1 shows an example of a scoring convention.

It is the responsibility of the designer constructing the evaluation trees for each snippet to conditionally allocate score so that the tree will produce a value within the appropriate dynamic range. In *DA:I*, each class of action uses a different set of scoring logic assets, built to return score values within the appropriate range. For example, the evaluation tree for a "Support" action starts by granting a baseline 25 points and conditionally adds contextual score up to a maximum of 45.

7.4.2 Target Selection

Most abilities in *DA:I* require a target to function. For example, an AI character cannot simply "cast Immolate"—they must cast Immolate *on* a specific foe. The chosen target of an ability can greatly affect the outcome (i.e., the utility value) of executing that ability. Consider: Casting Immolate on a target who is weak against fire will deal significant damage, whereas casting it on a target who is fire-immune will do nothing but waste mana. For that reason, target selection is a necessary part of the evaluation step; to accurately represent the value of an action, we must consider all the potential targets of that action, and then select the target which provides the greatest utility value. Therefore, in the BDS framework, evaluation trees return not only a score, but a target too.

The contextual nature of evaluation trees allows us to add target selection logic by introducing a "target selector" node. This node iterates over a list of designer-specified

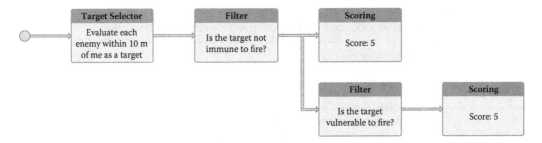

Figure 7.2

This evaluation tree specifically targets hostiles who are not immune to fire. Targets who are vulnerable to fire are scored higher than those who are not.

targets, and evaluates and assigns a score to each of them separately. Figure 7.2 shows an evaluation tree which makes use of the target selector node.

The target selector node maintains its own temporary evaluation state and record table, and executes according to the following algorithm:

1. Record the evaluation context's current score value as the "initial score."
2. For each targetable specified by the iterator data:
   a. Reset the context's score value to the initial score.
   b. Set the context's "behavior target iterator" slot to the current targetable.
   c. Evaluate the child node.
   d. If the child node returns true, record the context's current score value for the iterator's current targetable.
3. If at least one targetable has been recorded with an evaluation score:
   a. Set the context's Behavior Target slot to the targetable with the highest score.
   b. Set the context's score value to the score associated with that targetable.
   c. Return true.
4. If no targetables were recorded with an evaluation score, return false.

In this way, multiple targets are compared and only the target that generates the highest score for each snippet is associated with that snippet in the main BDS evaluation table.

7.4.3 Comparing Snippets

As part of the AI character's update, the evaluation tree for each registered behavior snippet is run, and the score & target produced by that tree is stored along with the snippet in a summary table. When all of the evaluation trees have been run, the snippet with the highest recorded score is selected to be executed. This cycle is typically repeated on every AI update pass, but can be performed as often as appropriate. Listing 7.1 contains a pseudocode implementation of this evaluation step.

It is not strictly necessary to retain any of the per-snippet evaluation results beyond the scope of the evaluation step; the execution step requires only a reference to the highest priority snippet and the selected targetable. In practice, though, we found that retaining the evaluation results in a debug-viewable table provides great insights when debugging and iterating on AI behavior.

```
struct SnippetEvaluation
{
    BehaviorSnippet snippet;
    Boolean result;
    Integer score;
    Character target;
};

// This function evaluates registered behaviors
// and returns the one with the highest utility.
Optional<SnippetEvaluation> EvaluateSnippets()
{
    list<SnippetEvaluation> evaluatedSnippets;
    for (BehaviorSnippet snippet: registeredBehaviors)
    {
        SnippetEvaluation evaluation = snippet.evaluate();
        if (evaluation.result == true)
            evaluatedSnippets.push(evaluation);
    }

    sortByDescendingScore(evaluatedSnippets);
    if (evaluatedSnippets.empty() == false)
        return evaluatedSnippets.first();
    else
        return None;
}
```

7.5 Execution Step

Having identified the highest scoring snippet, and a target for its associated ability, the final step is to execute that snippet. Just as each snippet contains an evaluation tree to show how the behavior should be evaluated, it also contains a behavior tree (termed the "execution tree") to show how the behavior should be executed. The execution tree is responsible for including any preparation or positioning required before performing the animation and game logic for the effective part of the action: the "active execution" of the action.

Like evaluation trees, execution trees have access to contextual information when being executed. Specifically, the BDS exposes information about the target which was selected during the evaluation step and the ability that the snippet is associated with. In order to simplify our execution trees, we defined a task node called "Execute Ability" which simply triggers the AI character to use the contextually-specified ability against the contextually-specified target. Figure 7.3 shows a typical "move-into-range-and-strike" execution tree.

Storing information about the ability and the target in the context (rather than explicitly referencing them in the execution tree) allows execution trees to remain generic, thus enabling their reuse across several different snippets. For example, the execution tree shown in Figure 7.3 could be applied to a punching attack, a stabbing attack, or a biting attack—just as long as the behavior occurs at melee range.

The execution tree belonging to the behavior snippet selected during the previous BDS evaluation pass will be executed once every AI update pass until the "Execute Ability"

Task	Filter	Execute ability
Set my movement behavior to move towards the target	Is my target within melee range?	Use the ability stored within the context against the target

Figure 7.3

This execution tree handles moving to achieve range and line-of-sight before executing a ranged attack and stopping movement.

node is fired, signaling that the execution of the behavior is complete. However, even while an AI character is executing a particular snippet, it is still desirable for the BDS to continue performing the evaluation step. Reevaluating in this way allows AI characters to execute new snippets in response to changing circumstances rather than mindlessly carrying out a previously selected snippet which has since become suboptimal. In fact, the contract between evaluation and execution logic is that the evaluation tree is responsible for identifying and guarding against any conditions which would make it impossible to fulfill the directives contained within the execution tree. In circumstances where an execution tree has become impossible to complete (e.g., if the target of the execution dies before the ability can be used) then reevaluation ensures that the now-invalid snippet will be replaced with a valid one. Having said that, once an AI character triggers the "Execute Ability" node, it is reasonable to suspend AI updates until the ability finishes executing; this minimizes wasted AI decisions that cannot be fulfilled while the character is occupied.

7.6 Movement and Passive Behaviors

Although the BDS was originally designed to prioritize, prepare, and execute discrete actions, in the course of developing *DA:I*, we discovered that the BDS evaluation-execution framework is also useful for regulating ongoing or "passive" behaviors.

For example, in *DA:I* if the player's AI-controlled allies have nothing else to do, they will simply follow the player, wherever he or she goes. This was incorporated into the BDS by registering a snippet whose evaluation tree simply returned a constant score lower than any action (e.g., a score of 0 in the context of the scoring system in Table 7.1) and whose execution tree does nothing but trigger the "follow the leader" movement behavior. This snippet is automatically invoked by the BDS when it becomes the character's highest priority (i.e., when no other snippets with scores of greater than 0 are viable.)

Further application of this approach allows us to use the BDS to choose between contextually appropriate movement behaviors by conditionalizing scoring logic just as we do for combat abilities. *DA:I* uses this approach to apply variations on the follower behavior if the party is in combat, or if the player has commanded a party member to remain at a certain location; these evaluate conditionally to higher priorities than the basic party movement while still yielding to active actions.

It can also be useful to create behavior snippets which conditionally exhibit extremely high priorities, as this will suppress the execution of any other actions that might otherwise be viable. *DA:I* uses this method on characters who are expected to remain within a certain "tethered" area. For these characters, we created a behavior snippet whose execution tree simply forces the AI character to return to the center of their assigned area. The corresponding evaluation tree returns a score higher than any other combat ability—but only when the character is positioned outside their assigned area. In this way, we ensure that if an AI character strays too far from their assigned position, they will always disengage from their current target and return home rather than allowing themselves to be drawn further and further away.

7.7 Modularity and Opportunities for Reuse

Through its use of behavior snippets, the BDS emphasizes a modular approach to AI design. A modular approach offers several benefits. When debugging, it allows developers to easily isolate the evaluation logic for a specific behavior, or to compare an AI character's relative priorities by examining the results of the evaluation step.

The modular design also allows behaviors to easily be shared or moved between AI characters and archetypes. *DA:I* leverages this functionality to allow human players to customize their AI-controlled party members. Throughout the game, the player can add, remove and modify AI characters' equipment and abilities. By tying behavior snippets to equipment and ability assets, and by following a consistent scoring system (as described in Section 7.4.1) we can ensure that AI characters will be able to make effective use of the equipment and abilities at their command—regardless of what those may be.

Although the desire for modularity was initially driven by the requirements of our AI-controlled allies, the benefits extend to hostile AI characters too. During the development of our hostile creature factions, we found that an ability or behavior which was developed for a specific AI character type could be easily shared with others, assuming that the relevant assets (e.g., animations and visual effects) also available for the new characters.

In order to support the modular design of the BDS, it is important to implement the evaluation and execution tree data structures so that they can be authored once and reused across multiple behavior snippets. In developing *DA:I*, we found that most behavior snippets could be implemented using a small pool of frequently-reused tree assets, whereas only a small number of complex actions required specific evaluation or execution logic. Modular decomposition and content-reuse can be promoted even further by separating commonly-recurring subtrees into standalone tree assets which can then be referenced from other trees. Consolidating scoring logic in this fashion can help reduce the ongoing maintenance cost of implementing a standardized scoring system.

7.8 Conclusion

In this chapter, we have presented the Behavior Decision System: a simple but powerful framework developed to support AI decision-making. At the core of the BDS are "behavior snippets"—data structures which encapsulate the information required to both evaluate and execute a discrete action. Snippets are both evaluated and executed using behavior trees; "evaluation trees" are modified behavior trees, which return both a utility score and a target, whereas execution trees contain the necessary instructions to carry out the action.

At runtime, behavior snippets can be registered to AI characters via the BDS, with each registered snippet representing a single action that the character can perform. By evaluating these snippets as part of the character's update loop and regularly executing the snippet which yields the greatest utility score, the BDS produces patterns of behavior which are directed, purposeful, and reactive.

Acknowledgments

The authors would like to thank Darren Ward who implemented the behavior tree system on which the BDS is based, along with Jenny Lee and Chris Dalton who adapted Darren's system to the Frostbite engine.

References

Graham, D. 2014. An introduction to utility theory. In *Game AI Pro: Collected Wisdom of Game AI Professionals*, ed. S. Rabin. Boca Raton, FL: CRC Press, pp. 113–126.

Merrill, B. 2014. Building utility decisions into your existing behavior tree. In *Game AI Pro: Collected Wisdom of Game AI Professionals*, ed. S. Rabin. Boca Raton, FL: CRC Press, pp. 127–136.

8

Paragon Bots
A Bag of Tricks

Mieszko Zieliński

8.1　Introduction

Paragon is a MOBA-type game developed by Epic Games, built with Unreal Engine 4 (UE4). Relatively late in the project a decision was made to add AI-controlled players (a.k.a. bots) into the game. Limited time and human resources, and the fact that crucial game systems had already been built around human players, meant there was no time to waste. Redoing human-player-centric elements was out of the question, so the only way left to go was to cut corners and use every applicable trick we could come up with. This chapter will describe some of the extensions we made to the vanilla UE4 AI systems as well as some of the simple systems tailored specifically for *Paragon* player bots. In the end, we added a few enhancements to our basic behavior tree implementation, came up with a few useful MOBA-specific spatial representations, integrated all of those with our mature spatial decision-making system, the environment query system (EQS), and added a few other tricks. The results exceeded our expectations!

8.2 Terms Primer

There are a number of terms in this chapter that might be unknown to the reader, so we will explain them here.

In *Paragon*, players control heroes. A *hero* is a character on a team that can use *abilities* to debuff or deal damage to enemy characters and structures, or to buff his or hers own teammates. Buffing means improving capabilities (like regeneration, movement or attack speed, and so on) whereas debuffing has an opposite effect. Abilities use up hero's *energy*, which is a limited resource. Abilities also use up time, in a sense, since they are gated by cooldowns. Some abilities are always active, whereas others require explicit activation. The goal of the game is to destroy the enemy's base, while protecting your own team's base. Defending access to the base are *towers* which teams can use to stop or slow advancing enemies. The towers are chained into paths called *lanes*. A lane is what *minions* use to move from one team's base to the other's. Minions are simple creatures that fight for their team, and they are spawned in *waves* at constant intervals.

There is more to the game than that; there is jungle between lanes, inhabited by jungle creeps (neutral creatures that heroes kill for experience and temporary buffs), where *experience wells* can be found. There is the hero and ability leveling up, and cards that provide both passive and active abilities, and much more. However, this chapter will focus only on how bots wrapped their heads around game elements described in the previous paragraph.

8.3 Extremely Parameterized Behavior Trees

An experienced AI developer might be surprised that all *Paragon* bots use the same behavior tree. With the time and resources constraints we were under, we could not afford to develop separate trees for every hero, or even every hero type. This resulted in a specific approach: The master behavior tree defines the generic structure, specifying the high-level order of behaviors, but details of behavior execution (like which ability to use, which spatial query to perform, and so on) are parameterized so that runtime values are polled from the AI agent when needed.

8.3.1 Vanilla UE4 Behavior Trees

Before we get into details of how Vanilla UE4 Behavior Trees (BTs) were used and expanded in *Paragon*, here is a quick overview. Since BTs have been in AI programmers' toolkit for years (Isla 2005) the description will be limited to what the UE4 implementation adds to the concept.

UE4 BTs are an event-driven approach to generic BTs. Once a leaf node representing a task is picked the tree will not reevaluate until the task is finished or conditions change. Execution conditions are implemented in the form of *decorator* nodes (Champandard 2007). When its condition changes, a decorator node may abort lower priority behaviors or its own subtree, depending on the setup.

The UE4 BT representation is closely tied to UE4's Blackboard (BB). In UE4, the blackboard is an AI's default generic information storage. It takes the form of a simple key-value pair store. It is flexible (it can store practically any type of information) and has a lot of convenient built-in features. Blackboards are dynamic in nature and are populated by data at runtime. BB entries are the easiest way to parameterize behavior tree nodes; it makes it possible for a BT node requiring some parameters to read the values from a blackboard entry indicated by a named key. BT decorator nodes can register with BB to observe specific entries and react to stored value changes in an event-driven fashion. BB entries are also used to parametrize BT nodes. One example of parametrized BT nodes is the *MoveTo* node, which gets the move goal location from a blackboard entry.

Our BT implementation has one more auxiliary node type—the *service* node. It is a type of node that is attached to a regular node (composite or leaf) and is "active" as long as its parent node is part of the active tree branch. A service node gets notification on being activated and deactivated, and has an option to tick at an arbitrary rate.

8.3.2 Environment Querying System

In UE4, the EQS is the AI's spatial querying solution and is mentioned here since it is mostly used by the BTs to generate and use runtime spatial information. EQS is used for tasks such as AI positioning and target selection (Zielinski 2013). EQS' queries are built in the UE4 editor, using a dedicated tool, and are stored as reusable templates. The vanilla UE4 BT supplies a task node and a service node for running EQS queries and storing the results in the blackboard.

For *Paragon*, we made changes to the EQS so that it would be possible to point at a query template we want to use by specifying a key in the blackboard. The query templates themselves are regular UE4 UObjects, so no work on the blackboard side was required. The only thing that needed to be done was to extend the BT task that issues environmental queries to be able to use query templates indicated by blackboard values. We then used this new feature to implement different positioning queries for melee and ranged heroes; melee heroes want to be very close to enemies when attacking, whereas ranged ones (usually) want to be at their abilities' range while keeping their distance so that the enemy does not get too close.

8.3.3 Blackboard Extension

Allowing the blackboard to store a new type is as simple as implementing a dedicated BB key type. For *Paragon* we added a dedicated key type for storing an *ability handle*, a value that uniquely identifies an ability the given hero could perform. With the new blackboard key type, we gained an easy way to configure BT nodes to use abilities picked for different purposes. Section 8.4 describes the way abilities are picked.

8.3.4 Behavior Moods

It is easy to think about the behavior tree as the final consumer of AI knowledge. The BT takes the data and decides on the best behavior, based on that knowledge. We do, however, have additional subsystems that need information regarding what is going on in the BT. It is not really about what the BT is doing specifically, just what its current "mood" is. We need to know if the bot is running away, attacking characters, attacking towers, and so on.

The current mood is set through a dedicated service node. The mood information is then used by some of the native code that is doing derived work, like setting AI agent's focus or deciding which movement-related abilities are allowed.

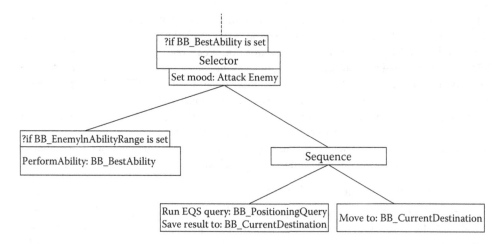

Figure 8.1

Example behavior tree branch controlling use of offensive abilities.

An example of how the described extensions and features mix together is shown in Figure 8.1. Names prefixed with BB indicate blackboard entries.

8.4 Ability Picker and Bot Ability Usage Markup

Deciding which ability to use in a given context, against a given target, is not a trivial task. The decision depends on multiple factors, like the target type, what we want to do to it, how much energy we have available at the moment, and which abilities are on cooldown. In addition, many abilities have multiple different effects. For example, there are abilities that damage or slow enemies, but they may also heal friendly heroes.

Abilities in *Paragon* are defined in UE4's Blueprint visual scripting language. This gives designers great flexibility in terms of how exactly each ability executes its behavior. Although this is great for content creator iteration and expressing creativity, it makes it practically impossible to extract the ability's usage information automatically. Besides, raw information about an ability is not enough to figure out how and when it makes sense to use it. To address that, we came up with a family of tags that designers used to mark up every ability an AI is supposed to use. We called those *bot ability usage* tags; examples are shown in Table 8.1.

Table 8.1 Examples of Bot Ability Usage Tags

BotAbilityUsage.Target.Hero	Use given ability to target heroes.
BotAbilityUsage.Effect.Damage	Given ability will damage the target.
BotAbilityUsage.Effect.Buff.Shield	Given ability will give the target a shield.
BotAbilityUsage.Mobility.Evade	Given ability can be used to evade enemy attack.

8.4.1 Ability Cached Data

When a bot-controlled hero is granted an ability, we digest the ability's blueprint to extract information useful for the AI. We store the results in the bot's *Ability Cached Data*, putting a lot of care into making sure the data representation is efficient. Ability usage tags get digested and represented internally as a set of flags. Other information stored includes the ability's range, type, damage, energy use, cooldown length, and so on. It also caches timestamps indicating when the given ability's cooldown will be over and when AI will have enough energy to cast the given ability. Every active ability available to a bot-controlled hero has its representation in the ability cache. Ability cached data is the key to the Ability Picker's efficiency.

8.4.2 Ability Picker

The *Ability Picker* is a simple yet surprisingly powerful service that is responsible for picking the right ability from a set of given abilities, given a certain target. The way the Ability Picker does that is extremely simple—actually, all the magic is already contained in the way the data is digested and stored as *ability cached data*. All the Ability Picker does is iterate through the list of abilities usable at a given point in time and checks if it matches the desired effect and target type. The returned ability is the one of "best cost" among the ones applicable. "Best cost" can have different meanings depending on the target type. When targeting minions, we prefer cheaper abilities, whereas we save the more expensive ones to target the heroes. Needless to say this scoring approach leaves a lot of room for improvement.

The core Ability Picker algorithm is extremely straightforward and is presented in pseudocode in Listing 8.1.

Listing 8.1. Ability Picker's core algorithm.

```
FindAbilityForTarget(AIAgent, InTargetData, InDesiredEffects)
{
    BestAbility = null;

    for Ability in AIAgent.AllAbilities:
        if Ability.IsValidTarget(InTargetData)
            && (Ability.DesiredEffects & InDesiredEffects)
            && (Ability.CooldownEndTimestamp < CurrentTime)
            && (Ability.EnoughEnergyTimestamp < CurrentTime):
                Score = Ability.RequiredEnergy;
                if IsBetterScore(InTargetData, Score, BestScore):
                    BestScore = Score;
                    BestAbility = Ability;

    return BestAbility;
}
```

`AllAbilities` is an array containing ability cached data of every ability available to the bot. The `IfValidTarget` function checks if a given target is of an appropriate type (Hero, Minion, Tower), if it is of a valid team, and if the target's *spatial density* (described below) is high enough. `IsBetterScore`, as mentioned above, prefers lower scores for minions and higher scores for heroes, so that we go cheap while fighting minions and wait to unload on heroes.

8.4.3 Target's Spatial Density

Some abilities are tagged by designers as usable against minions, but it makes sense to use them only if there is more than one minion in the area. This applies to *Area-of-Effect* abilities (AoE), which affect multiple targets in a specified area rather than a single target. Using such an ability on a single minion is simply a waste of energy and time.

To be able to efficiently test if a given target is "alone," we find *Spatial Density* for every target we pass to the Ability Picker. Target density is calculated as part of influence map calculations, which is described later in this chapter, so getting this information at runtime is a matter of a simple lookup operation.

8.4.4 Debugging

Having one system to control all ability selection had an added benefit of being easier to debug. It was very easy to add optional, verbose logging that once enabled would describe which abilities were discarded during the selection process, and why. The logged information combined with the spatial and temporal context we get out of the box with UE4's Visual Log allowed us to quickly solve many ability selection problems—which usually turned out to be bugs in ability markup. You can never trust those darn humans!

A handy trick that proved invaluable during bots' ability execution testing was adding a console command used at game runtime to override ability selection to always pick the specified ability. Thanks to the centralized approach we were able to implement it by plugging a piece of debugging logic into Ability Picker's `FindAbilityForTarget` function that would always pick the specified ability.

8.5 One-Step Influence Map

The influence map is a concept well known in game AI; it has been around for many years (Tozour 2001). It is a very simple concept, easy to grasp, straightforward to set up, but produces great, useful data from the very simple information it is being fed. The idea is based on a notion that units exert a "spatial influence" on their environment, proportional to their strength, health, combat readiness, or anything else that decays with distance. The influence map is a superposition of all those influences and can be used to guide AI decisions.

Normally, building an influence map involves every agent going through two steps. First is to apply the agent's influence at the agent's current location. This usually is the place where the agent has the highest influence (although there are other possibilities [Dill 2015]). The second step is influence propagation. We take the given agent's influence and propagate it to all neighboring areas, and then to areas neighboring those areas, and so on. The agent's influence distributed this way is a function of distance—the further from the source, the weaker the influence is.

Influence propagation can be a very expensive operation; depending on the influence map representation and resolution (although there are algorithms supplying infinite-resolution influence maps [Lewis 2015]). Also, it gets even more expensive the more influence sources we consider. Due to the constraints on processing for *Paragon* servers, the naive approach was not chosen.

There are multiple ways to represent an influence map. Performance is very important to *Paragon* bots, so we went for a very simple structure to represent influence on our maps. Since there is no gameplay-relevant navigable space overlaps on the vertical axis, we were able to represent the map with a simple 2D cell grid, with every cell representing a fixed-size square of the map. The size of the square used was a compromise between getting high-resolution data and not taking too much memory to store the map or using too much CPU when calculating influence updates. After some experimentation, we settled on using cells of 5×5 m which was a good compromise between memory requirements (320 kB for the whole map) and tactical movement precision. In addition, we have auxiliary information associated with every cell where we store influence source's counters that are used in multiple ways. More on that later.

We cannot simply ignore the fact that different enemies have different range and strength properties, that would affect the influence map naturally with influence propagation. In lieu of actual influence propagation, we apply influence of some agents to map cells in a certain radius rather than just in the one cell where the agent is currently present. We used zero radius for every minion (even the ranged ones) and for heroes we used every given hero's primary ability range. One could argue that applying influence in a radius rather than a point is almost the same as influence propagation, but there is a substantial performance gain when applying the influence to every cell in a radius compared to propagating it to consecutive neighbors, especially if the propagation would care about cell-to-cell connectivity. Applying influence to all cells in a radius does have a side effect of ignoring obstacles that would normally block influence, but due to the dynamics of *Paragon* matches and the way *Paragon* maps are built, this effect is negligible.

The main way we wanted to use the influence map was to determine bot positioning in combat. Depending on the hero type and situation, we might want a bot to keep away from enemies (the default case for ranged heroes), or on the contrary, keep close to enemies (the default for melee heroes). We can also use "friendly influence" as an indication of safer locations, or the opposite, to help bots spread out to avoid being easy AoE attack targets. It turns out that influence propagation is not really required for the described use cases because the influence range, defined as heroes' effective range, is already embedded into influence map data. Propagated data would give us some knowledge regarding how the tactical situation may change, but in *Paragon* it changes all the time, so we went for a cheaper solution over the one that would produce only subtly better results. Influence propagation can also be faked to a degree by deliberately extending the radius used for every hero. The extension can even be derived from runtime information, like current speed, amount of health, energy, and so on, because we build the influence map from scratch on a regular basis.

As will be discussed below, the influence map integrates with EQS to impact spatial processes like positioning, target selection, and so on.

8.5.1 Other Influence Sources

Other game actor types can also alter the influence map. Let us first consider towers (defensive structures described in Section 8.2). All characters entering an enemy tower's attack range are in serious danger, since towers pack a serious punch, even to high-level heroes. However, influence information is being used only by hero bots, and heroes are safe inside enemy tower range as long as the hero is accompanied by minions—minions are the primary target for towers. For this reason, we include a given tower's influence information in the map building only if the tower has no minions to attack; otherwise the bot does not care about the tower danger (or in fact, even know about it!).

One thing worth mentioning here is that since towers are static structures we do not need to recalculate which influence map cells will be affected every frame. Instead, we gather all the influenced cells at the start of the match and then just reuse that cached information whenever we rebuild the influence map.

One other influence source we consider during influence map building is AoE attacks. Some of those attacks persist long enough for it to make sense to include them in influence calculations. Having that information in the influence map makes it easy to "see" the danger of going into such an area! We do not annotate the influence map with short-lasting AoE attacks since the AI would not have a chance to react to them anyway—those attacks last just long enough to deal damage and there is practically no chance to avoid them once they are cast.

8.5.2 Information Use

As stated previously, the main use of the influence information is for bot positioning. This information is easily included in the rest of positioning logic by adding another test type expanding our spatial querying system (EQS). Thanks to EQS test mechanics, a single test that is simply reading influence information from specified locations in the world can be used to both score and filter locations a bot would consider as potential movement goals. Incorporating this one simple test into all bots' positioning queries allowed us to get really good results quickly. Thanks to this change, bots gained the power to avoid entering enemy towers' fire or running into groups of enemies and to pick locations close to friends, and so on.

Recall the auxiliary information associated with every cell of the map. That information is not strictly part of the influence map, but it is gathered as part of influence map building. The auxiliary information includes a list of agents influencing each cell. We use this information to improve the performance of minions' perception by effectively reducing the number of targets they consider for regular line-of-sight tests. Querying the influence map for enemy minions or heroes in a given area boils down to a simple lookup operation.

One last bit of influence-derived data is something we called *target density*. It is a simple per-cell counter of enemies of a given type (minion or hero), and we use that to determine if a given target is "alone" or if we would potentially hit some other targets when attacking the specific considered target. This is the information that hints to the Ability Picker whether using an AoE ability on a given target would be a waste of *energy* or not.

This kind of creative data reuse was necessary due to our time restrictions. We spent time building a system, so then we had to squeeze as much from it as possible.

8.6 Lane Space

A question we often had to answer was "how far bot X is from Y in terms of the lane it is on," where Y could be an enemy tower, a hero, a minion wave, or just an arbitrary location in the world. We did not really care about actual 3D distance, just about "how far along

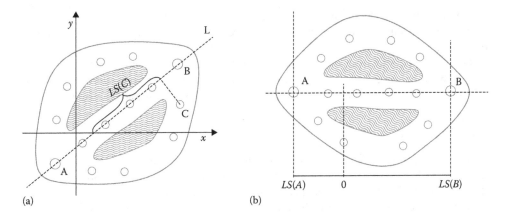

Figure 8.2

(a) A traditional MOBA map. (b) Map transformed to align with one of the axes.

the lane" things were. This is extremely easy to answer if lanes are straight lines, but that is not quite the case in *Paragon*... unless we straighten them out!

Figure 8.2a depicts a regular MOBA map, where A and B mark locations of both teams' bases. There are three lanes, with left and right lanes being not at all straight. This is where the concept of *Lane Space* comes in. Transforming a 3D world location into the lane space is a matter of projecting it to the line defined by $\overline{AB}$ segment. See Figure 8.2b for an illustration of this transformation.

Introducing lane space made it easy to add a new type of EQS test for scoring or filtering based on relative distance to the combat line on a given lane. We used it for example to make ranged bots prefer locations 10 meters behind the minions.

8.6.1 Lane Progress

A natural extension of the lane space is the idea of *Lane Progress*. It is a metric defined as a location's lane space distance from A or B, normalized by $|\overline{AB}|$ (distance from A to B). Lane progress is calculated in relation to a given team's base, so for example for team A lane progress value of base A location would be 0, and base B location would be 1. For team B it is the other way around; in fact, for every team A's lane progress value of x, the value for team B will be equal to $(1 - x)$.

8.6.2 Front-Line Manager

It is important in a MOBA for heroes to understand positioning in a lane based on areas of danger and safety. In combat, the ranged heroes prefer staying a bit behind the minion line, whereas melee heroes should be at the front-line, where the brawling takes place.

To allow the bots to behave like real humans do, we created the Front-Line Manager. Its sole purpose is to track all the minions left alive, along with all the remaining towers, and calculate where the lane's combat is. The Front-Line Manager is being fed information regarding minions by the influence map manager during influence map building. Based on that information and on the current state of a given team's towers on every lane, the Front-Line Manager is calculating the *front-line* on every lane for both teams. The exact front-line value is expressed in terms of lane progress.

Similarly, to the influence map information, we incorporate front-line information into the positioning logic by implementing another EQS test that measures locations' distance to the front-line.

One other place the front-line information is relevant is during enemy selection. We want to avoid bots chasing enemy heroes too deep into the enemy territory, so the distance from the front-line contributes to target scoring. Again, this is done with a dedicated EQS test.

8.7 Other Tricks

Cutting corners was crucial due to time constraints, so there is a fair amount of other, smaller tricks we used. Those are usually simple temporary solutions that either work well enough so that players would not notice, or are placeholders for solutions that will come in the future.

The first one worth mentioning is *perfect aim*. The ranged hero bots aim exactly at their target's location. This is not strictly speaking cheating, since experienced players do not have a problem doing the same. And it is not even as deadly as it sounds, since most ranged abilities used physical projectiles (meaning the hits are not instant) and some of them have ballistic properties (meaning they obey gravity). It is not a problem to add a slight aim angle deviation; *Paragon*'s easy-difficulty bots actually do that, it is just that the "perfect aim" helps revision-one bots to bridge the skill gap to human players. Besides, there are so many things humans have brain-hardware support for (especially visual processing), why should bots give up one of the few things bots are born with!

Another simple trick we used was to address a complaint we got from people playing in mixed human-bot teams. The problem was that as soon as the game started, all the bots were taking off to race down the lanes. It was suggested that bots should wait a bit, for example until minion waves started spawning. Since that would be a one-time behavior, considering it as a part of regular AI reasoning would be a waste of performance. Good old *scripted behavior* came to the rescue. We came up with a very simple idea (and implementation) of a one-time behavior that is triggered at the beginning of the match. It makes bots wait for minions to spawn and then *flow* down the lanes until they've seen an enemy, or reached the middle of the map, at which point bots simply switch over to the default behavior. *Flowing* down the lane involves using *Paragon*'s custom navigation flow-field, which makes movement fully pathfinding-free, and thus a lot cheaper than regular AI navigation. Once we had scripted behavior support, it came in useful in testing as well.

8.8 Conclusion

I feel that working on game AI is an art of using what is available and coming up with simple solutions to usually not-so-simple problems. In the chapter we've shown how this approach has been applied to work done on *Paragon* bots. Reusing and extending your AI systems is especially crucial when working under heavy time pressure, so investing effort ahead of time to make those systems flexible will pay off in the future. Using a single behavior tree for all bots in *Paragon* would not be possible otherwise. When it comes to solving game-specific problems, it is usually best to come up with a simple solution that isolates the problem and hides the complexity from the rest of AI code by supplying some easy-to-comprehend abstraction. The Ability Picker and Front-Line Manager are great examples of this. The "Keep It Simple" rule is always worth following!

References

Champandard, A., Behavior trees for Next-Gen AI, *Game Developers Conference Europe*, Cologne, Germany, 2007.

Dill, K., Spatial reasoning for strategic decision making. In *Game AI Pro 2: Collected Wisdom of AI Professionals*, ed. S. Rabin. Boca Raton, FL: A. K. Peters/CRC Press, 2015.

Isla, D., Handling complexity in the Halo 2 AI, *Game Developers Conference*, San Francisco, CA, 2005.

Lewis, M., Escaping the grid: Infinite-resolution influence mapping. In *Game AI Pro 2: Collected Wisdom of AI Professionals*, ed. S. Rabin. Boca Raton, FL: A. K. Peters/CRC Press, 2015.

Tozour, P., Influence mapping. In *Game Programming Gems 2*, ed. M. Deloura. Hingham, MA: Charles River Media, 2001.

Zielinski, M., Asking the environment smart questions. In *Game AI Pro: Collected Wisdom of AI Professionals*, ed. S. Rabin. Boca Raton, FL: A. K. Peters/CRC Press, 2013.

9

Using Your Combat AI Accuracy to Balance Difficulty

Sergio Ocio Barriales

9.1 Introduction

In a video game, tweaking combat difficulty can be a daunting task. This is particularly true when we talk about scenarios with multiple AI agents shooting at the player at the same time. In such situations, unexpected damage spikes can occur, which can make difficulty balancing harder. This chapter will show how to avoid them without compromising the player experience and while still giving designers lots of affordances for balancing.

There are a few different ways to deal with this problem. We could adjust the damage AI weapons do; we could add some heuristics that dynamically modify damage values based on things such as the time elapsed since the player was last hit or the number of AIs that are simultaneously targeting the player; or we could have AIs be less accurate and only really hit the player once every few shots.

The latter will be our focus for this chapter: Playing with AIs' accuracy to achieve better control over the amount of damage the player can receive each frame. This is a complicated and interesting topic, with two main parts:

1. What algorithm is used to decide when it is time to hit the player? How many agents can hit the player simultaneously?
2. How can we make our AIs not look ridiculous or unrealistic when they are purposely missing or holding off their shots?

9.2 Damage Dynamics

In an action game, difficulty level is usually related to how likely the player is to die during a game, or to the amount of experience required to progress through the experience (Suddaby 2013). Depending on the design of the game the way we control this can change. For example, in a first-person shooter we can decide to make enemies more aggressive, carry more powerful weapons, or simply spawn a higher enemy count; or, in a survival game, we could reduce the ammunition a player will find scattered through the world.

Adjusting how challenging a video game experience should be is normally a long and costly process in which different teams collaborate to improve the final player experience (Aponte et al. 2009). Programmers will expose new parameters for designers to tweak, enemy placement will change, levels will continue evolving and things will be tested over and over until the game is released ... and beyond!

Let us focus on the average cover shooter game. Normally, in these games, a few enemies will take covered positions that give them line-of-sight on the player. AIs will move around the level to try and find better firing locations if their positions are compromised or if they lose line-of-sight on their target, and they will unload their clips at the player, taking breaks for weapon reloading to add some variety to their behaviors. Combat will usually continue until (a) every AI is killed, (b) the player is killed, or (c) the target is not detected anymore.

In a scenario like this, one of the easiest ways to control difficulty, providing we keep enemy count constant, would be playing with damage dynamics, that is, adjusting the amount of damage inflicted by the AI when the player is hit (Boutros 2008). This is not a complex method in terms of the programming involved, but it requires lots of tweaking by designers.

Although this is a good strategy, it also has its problems. For instance, we could still face the problem of multiple AIs potentially shooting and hitting the player at the same time. This is solvable, for example, by tracking the total damage the target has received each frame and adjust incoming damage accordingly (e.g., not damaging the target anymore after a certain threshold has been hit), but this could lead to other believability problems; though solvable, the focus of this chapter is on a different type of solution, that we will talk about in the subsequent sections.

9.3 Token Systems

One way to address the one-hit kill syndrome is to have AIs take turns when attacking the player. This is commonly achieved by using a logical token that gets passed around the different agents involved in combat. Tokens can control different behaviors, but they basically fulfill the same purpose no matter what the action is: Only the AIs that hold a token will be able to execute the behavior. For example, we could decide that only AIs with a token can fire their weapons. If we have, let us say, just one token for the whole game, this means one, and only one, AI will be able to shoot at any given point in time. When the shooting is done, the token holder will release it, and another agent will take a turn.

The problem is that since only one AI is allowed to use its weapon at a time this could yield potentially unbelievable behaviors, such as AIs being at perfect spots to shoot and hit the player but not even trying to do so because they are clearly waiting for their turn.

9.4 Dynamic Accuracy Control

Our goal is to control the difficulty of our game and offer players a fairer, less chaotic game. Token systems will help us achieve that, but we can still make some improvements to offer a more polished experience.

Let us change the rules we used in the previous section. Tokens will not gate the shooting behavior anymore; instead, AIs can freely enter any of the shooting behaviors, but shots can only actually hit the player if the shooter has a token; any other shot will deliberately miss the player and hit some location around him or her.

Token distribution is controlled by a global timer that tracks how long has passed since the last hit. But, how long should the delay between hits be? Players will understand agents are not so accurate if, for example, they are far from their targets. In that case, having a long delay between hits is not a problem. But missing shots can affect the believability of our AI if the target is clearly visible and in range. To try and have the best of both worlds—predictability over the damage the target is going to take and a believable behavior, we need to use a variable, dynamic delay between hits.

9.4.1 Calculating the Final Delay

To define this delay, we will start from a base value, and define a few rules that will generate multipliers for our base value, increasing or decreasing the final time between shots. The final delay will be calculated as:

$$\text{delay} = \text{delay}_{\text{base}} * \prod_{i=0}^{n} \text{rule}_i$$

Where rule_i is a floating-point value resulting of running one of our rules.

In this section we will simplify things and say that we are fighting a single AI agent—we will show how to deal with multiple agents in the next section. With this in mind, let us define a few rules and show what the delay would look like in a couple of different scenarios.

9.4.2 Rules and Multipliers

Our first rule is distance. We want players to feel more pressure if they are closer to the AI, so we will allow our agents to hit players more frequently the closer they are to their targets. For our example, we will say that any distance greater than 15 m will not affect the delay, and that anything closer than 5 m will halve the time. Figure 9.1 shows the function we will use to generate our multiplier based on distance.

For our second multiplier, we will check the current stance of the player. In this case, we will keep the base delay if the player is standing (i.e., the multiplier is 1), but double it

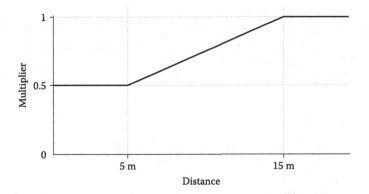

Figure 9.1

Our distance rule will generate a multiplier that will make the delay smaller the closer the player is to the AI.

if they are crouching, making the player feel safer. Likewise, we will use another rule that will double the delay if the player is in a valid cover position.

The current facing direction of the player is also an interesting factor. In this case, we can use it to be fairer and more forgiving with players if they are looking away from the AI, doubling the delay if the angle difference between the facing vector and the vector that goes from the player to the AI is greater than 170 degrees, and leaving the delay unchanged otherwise. Similarly, we can use the velocity of the player to check if they are trying to run away from the AI or toward our agents. Based on the angle between the velocity vector and, again, the vector that goes from the player to the AI, we will calculate a multiplier such as shown in Figure 9.2.

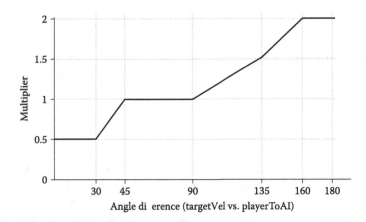

Figure 9.2

For our rule that takes into account target velocity, we have used a more complex curve to define how the multiplier is calculated.

9. Using Your Combat AI Accuracy to Balance Difficulty

For our example, this rule will halve the delay if the angle is lower than 30°, maintain it unchanged between 45° and 90° and make if longer the closer we get to 180° (we are actually capping it at 160°).

Finally, we could use other rules and multipliers, such as a rule based on the weapon the AI is wielding, but, for simplicity, we will not study these in this chapter.

9.4.3 Dynamic Delay Calculation Examples

With our rules defined, let us say our base delay is 0.5 s and define a first scenario in which the player is hiding, crouching behind cover 30 m away from the AI. With these constrains, we have:

- The distance multiplier is 1, since we are well over the 20 m cap.
- The stance of the player generates a multiplier of 2.
- Because the player is behind cover, we have another multiplier of 2. Also, since we are in cover, we will ignore the rest of the rules, as they are not applicable in this case (e.g. there is no player velocity, and we can consider the player facing is not relevant).

The final delay is $0.5 * (1*2*2) = 2 \ s.$

We will define a second scenario in which the player is out in the open, running toward the AI, 10 m away. Our rules would be yielding the following results:

- Based on distance, we have a multiplier of 0.75.
- The player is standing, which results in a multiplier of 1, and not behind cover, so that is another 1 for that rule.
- The player is looking at the AI and running toward it. Let us say that, in this case, both facing and velocity vectors are the same—they could be different if, for instance, the player was strafing—and the angle difference is very close to 0 degrees. This will generate a multiplier of 1 based on facing and the target velocity rule will calculate a 0.5 multiplier.

The delay for the second scenario is $0.5 * (0.75 * 1 * 1 * 1 * 0.5) = 0.1875 \ s.$

The dynamic delay will handle what the player is doing and increase—by allowing the AI to hit the player more frequently—or decrease difficulty accordingly. This system avoids multiple hits occurring on the same frame and can be tweaked by designers to balance the game in a way that is reactive to players' actions.

9.5 Dealing with Multiple AIs and Different Archetypes

In the previous section, we studied how our solution would work if we are dealing with a single enemy. However, this is normally not the case. Enemies will most likely be spawned in groups, and we can, as well, face different enemy types (archetypes). In this case, the algorithm remains very similar: We still use a single timer and we need to update its duration properly. The main difference is that, in the case of a single AI, all the calculations were made by applying our rules to that agent; when multiple AIs are present, we need to choose which should receive the token, and calculate the duration of the delay for that particular agent.

9.5.1 Selecting the Most Relevant Agent

Calculating which AI should get the token involves looking at a few different variables. Some of these are as follows:

- *Distance to the player:* The closer an agent is to the target the more options it has to receive a token.
- *Target exposure:* Depending on the position of the AI agent, the player can be more or less exposed to the attacks of the AI. For example, a cover position can be valid against a particular agent, but the same position can be completely exposed to an AI agent that is standing directly behind the player. The latter agent would have a better chance of obtaining the token.
- *Archetype:* The tougher the type of enemy, the easier it is for it to get the token.
- If an agent is currently under attack, it is more likely that it will receive the token.
- *Token assignment history:* Agents that have not received a token in a long time may have a higher chance of receiving the token soon.

A weighted sum will be used to combine these factors, generating a score for each actor. The actor with the highest score will be chosen as the most relevant agent. The weights we use can vary depending on the type of experience we want to offer. For example, if we had an enemy with a special weapon that generates some effect on the player that is really important for our game, we could use a very high weight for the archetype factor while using lower values for other ones. That way we would almost be guaranteeing that the special enemy will be the one hitting the player.

9.5.2 Dealing with Changes

Rechecking who is the most relevant agent every frame, we solve problems that are inherently common in action games, such as what happens if an AI reaches a better position, if the player keeps moving, or if an AI gets killed. Let us analyze a couple of scenarios.

In the first one, we have two agents, A and B. A is selected as the most relevant agent and the delay is 1s. The player runs toward B and starts shooting at it. The algorithm determines B is more relevant now since it is under attack and changes the selection. Also, because the player is running directly toward it, the facing and target velocity rules decide the delay should be shorter, so it is recalculated as 0.75 s. Time passes and the timer expires based on the new delay, so B hits the player, who turns around trying to retreat after being hit. A becomes the new selected AI and the delay goes back to 1 s. A second later, A hits the player.

For the second scenario, we have three agents—two regular soldiers (A and B) and a heavy soldier (C). C has just hit the player and now A is the most relevant AI. The delay for A is 2 s. After 1.5 s, A is killed. The algorithm determines C is, again, the most relevant AI, since it is in a better position than B and it is wielding a more powerful weapon. C is also a heavy, and the system calculates the delay is now 0.75 s. Since it has already been 1.5 s since the last hit, C gets a token immediately and the player is hit.

9.6 Improving Believability

If we want players to enjoy our game and our AI, we need to prevent breaking the suspension of disbelief (Woelfer 2016). In our case, this means hiding the processes that are happening behind the scenes—our damage control system—from players, so they are not distracted by the fact that the AI is being generous and missing shots on purpose to make the game more fun.

With this in mind, we have to take two points into consideration:

1. Although we normally communicate to the player he or she is being hit by using some HUD or VFX on the screen, we would completely lose that information if the player is not actually being hit.
2. Since most of the shots are going to miss the target, we need to make players not notice this fact.

9.6.1 Conveying Urgency

An important part of every game is that players understand the different situations they face and know how to identify and read the messaging the game provides about its systems and/or the state of the world.

If we stop hitting the player, we still need to produce a feeling of "being under pressure" when he or she is being targeted by an AI, in order to maintain engagement. We will mainly do this through sound effects and visual effects. For the former, 3D positioned sounds can help players pinpoint where shots are coming from, and also that some of them are missing the target; for visuals, we will use tracers and some VFX, like sparks or other particle effects.

9.6.2 Choosing Interesting Random Targets

If we want to make things interesting and good looking—so we can divert attention from the fact that the AI's accuracy is not very good—we need to ensure bullet hits will be seen by players and that they will clearly convey the player is under attack (Lidén 2003). This applies both to single shot weapons and automatic or semi-automatic ones; for the latter types, we could either calculate an interesting target for each bullet in the burst or, potentially, generate a single target and add some randomization around it or some special patterns, such as straight lines that the recoil of the weapon may be generating, to create better effects. The objective to keep in mind is that we are trying to polish the looks of things!

Let us refine the idea of picking random locations around the target, and ask ourselves: Are all these missed shots going to be noticed by the player? The answer is probably not. If we are just aiming at a random position in a circle around the target, as we show in Figure 9.3, the only thing players are going to notice for most of the shots is their tracers.

Instead, what we want is to make our "accuracy problems" an interesting situation from the visual standpoint, so what we should try to do is hit things surrounding the player to generate sparks, dust... in a nutshell, destruction. We still want to randomize our shots and fire the occasional one that does not hit anything, but we should try and minimize them.

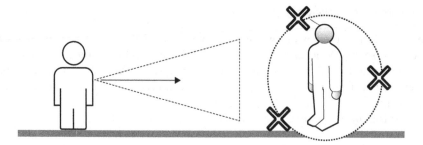

Figure 9.3

An AI that is consciously missing shots could target random positions around the enemy.

So, how do we choose better targets? In the average cover shooter, we will find that almost all scenarios fall in one of these three categories: Target is behind full cover, target is behind half cover, and target is out in the open. Let us analyze each of these individually.

9.6.2.1 Target Behind Full Cover

We call "full cover" anything that occludes the full height of the target. These are normally door sides, columns, pillars, and so on. Peeking out can only be done left and/or right, depending on which sides of the cover gives the user of the cover line-of-sight on its target. Figure 9.4 depicts this type of location.

If the target is behind full cover, we have two options. First, we can aim at positions near the ground next to the peek-out side of the cover; this are most likely going to be noticed by the player, since they are hitting the area he or she would have to use to leave the cover. Alternatively, we could also hit the cover directly, especially when the player is completely peeking out, as these hits are going to remind the player he or she can be hit at any point.

9.6.2.2 Target Behind Half Cover

A "half cover" is that which only occludes half of the height of the user, requiring him or her to crouch behind it to be fully protected. In this case, peeking out can also be done standing up and looking above the cover. Figure 9.5 shows this scenario.

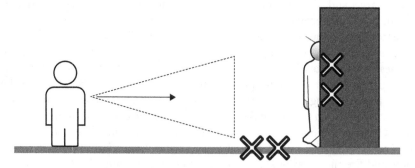

Figure 9.4

The AI's target is behind full cover, so we can target both the ground next to the cover and the cover itself.

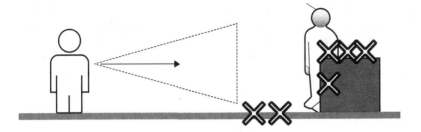

Figure 9.5

The AI's target is behind half cover, so we can target the ground next to the cover, the top of the cover and its side.

If the target is behind half cover, our options are similar to the ones we had in a full-cover situation. However, now we have an extra targetable area: the top of the cover. Most of our missed shots should aim at this zone, since they are closer to the eyes of the target, and thus, more likely to be seen.

9.6.2.3 Target Out in the Open

If our target is out in the open, the position we should choose is not as clear, and it depends on what the player is trying to do. For example, if the player is stationary, we could potentially shoot at the ground in front of the player, if this area is within camera view. But normally players will be moving around, so our best bet will be trying to whiz tracers right past the player's face at eye level.

9.6.3 Targeting Destructible Objects

Although we have presented some tricks to help choose the best random targets we can try to hit when we do not have the shooting token, we can always tag certain objects in the scene that are destructible and use them to create more spectacular and cinematic moments.

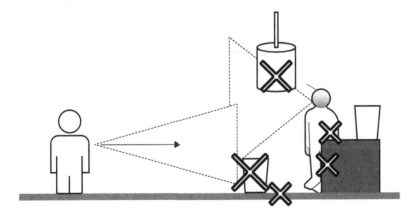

Figure 9.6

Destructible objects that are within the player's FOV should be targeted when our AI agents miss shots.

It is important to note that the destructibles we choose to target should also be in generally the same area as the player, if we want things to remain credible. Moreover, we should only target these special items if the player is going to see it, since these objects are limited in number and we should not waste the opportunity to use them. Figure 9.6 shows an area with destructible objects.

9.7 Conclusion

In this chapter, we have talked about different options to help make damage throughput more predictable, making it easier for designers to balance the game. But we also showed that, in order for our AI to look smart and believable, we need to control how the AI is going to deal with its targeting decisions.

Game AI is an art of smoke and mirrors—everything is permitted as long as we create a spectacular and fun experience. Tricks like playing with our AIs' accuracy can be used to control difficulty, and can help designers create better and more enjoyable games. It is our hope that readers can make use of these, or similar, techniques to keep improving what AI has to offer.

References

Aponte, M., Levieux, G., and Natkin, S. 2009. Scaling the level of difficulty in single player video games. In *Entertainment Computing–ICEC 2009*, eds. S. Natkin and J. Dupire. Berlin, Germany: Springer, 2009, pp. 24–35.

Boutros, D. Difficulty is difficult: Designing for hard modes in games. http://www.gamasutra.com/view/feature/3787/difficulty_is_difficult_designing_.php (accessed April 29, 2016).

Lidén, L. 2003. Artificial stupidity: The art of intentional mistakes. In *AI Game Programming Wisdom 2*, ed. S. Rabin. Rockland, MA: Charles River Media Inc.

Suddaby, P. Hard mode: Good difficulty versus bad difficulty. http://gamedevelopment.tutsplus.com/articles/hard-mode-good-difficulty-versus-bad-difficulty--gamedev-3596 (accessed May 9, 2016).

Woelfer, A. Suspension of disbelief|game studies. Video game close up. https://www.youtube.com/watch?v=Y2v3cOFNmLI (accessed May 9, 2016).

10

1000 NPCs at 60 FPS

Robert Zubek

10.1 Introduction

In this chapter we look at the AI used to implement characters in the game *Project Highrise* by SomaSim, a skyscraper construction management sim where players build, lease out, and manage a series of highrise buildings.

The AI goal in this simulation game was to implement a "living building," simulating the everyday lives of hundreds of inhabitants of the player's skyscraper, their daily lives and routines. As described in more detail in the next section, we gave ourselves a benchmark goal to hit: In order to meet gameplay needs, up to 1000 NPCs should be able to live in the player's building simultaneously, without dropping below 60 FPS on commodity hardware.

This chapter will describe how we approached the AI implementation that achieves this goal. We will first look at the game itself to illustrate the motivations and constraints behind the AI problem, then in the subsequent section, we will describe two action selection mechanisms we implemented (and why we settled on using just one of them), and following that, a performant system for actually executing these actions.

10.1.1 About the Game

Let us quickly introduce the game itself, as shown in Figure 10.1. The player's job in *Project Highrise* is to invest in the construction of highrise buildings, and then manage them successfully: Get tenants to move in, keep them happy, make sure everybody gets what

Figure 10.1

Screenshot from early game in *Project Highrise*.

they need, and pays rent on time. As in management simulation games of this type, the game board is populated by an ever-increasing variety and number of units, such as offices and restaurants renting space in the building, and characters going in and out of those units, going to work, getting lunch, coming home at night, and so on.

We will not go into further details on the gameplay or the economic simulation in the game, since they are beyond the scope of this chapter, except to point out that they all introduced a common goal: We needed the building to feel alive, to be filled with computer characters whose daily comings and goings would fill the building with irresistible bustle. In addition to the aesthetic feel of that, the NPCs' economic activity drives the economy of the building, which provides the main challenge for the player, so we needed the NPCs to be simulated on an ongoing basis instead of being simply instanced into view and then culled.

We gave ourselves a concrete performance goal: The game needed to be able to simulate and display 1000 NPCs, running at 60 FPS on a reasonably recent desktop-grade personal computer. Furthermore, there was a resource challenge: We were a tiny team, and we knew that during most of the development, we would only have one developer on staff whose job would involve not just AI, but also building *the entire rest of the game* as well. So we needed an AI system that was very fast to build, required very little ongoing maintenance once built—and primarily, helped us reach our performance goal.

Early on we decided to keep things very simple, and to split our character AI into two parts, with *action selection* driving decision-making, and separate *action performance module* acting on those orders.

10.2 Action Selection

Action selection is a fundamental decision process in character AI: What should I be doing at the given point in time? During the game's development, we actually tried two different implementations of action selection: first, a propositional planner, and second, a much simpler time-based scheduler of daily routine scripts.

The goal was to reproduce everyday human behavior: Office workers coming in to work in the morning, maybe taking a lunch break, and working at their desk most of the time until it is time to go home; apartment dwellers coming home in the evening and puttering about until bedtime; maintenance and janitorial crews doing their nightly work, whereas everybody else is sound asleep, and so on.

We did not have to worry too much about animation fidelity as the characters were just 2D sprites. Rather, our focus was on overall character behavior, because the actions of your residents and workers directly drive the in-game economy. For example, your food court restaurants need those office workers taking their lunch breaks so they can turn a profit, and you in turn depend on those restaurants paying rent, so you can recoup your investment. Character behavior is central to the economy core loop.

10.2.1 First System: A Propositional Planner

The planning system was our first stab at action selection for NPCs. This happened early in preproduction, and at that point we did not yet know how much "smarts" we would need or want from our characters, but we knew flexibility was crucial. Since the game simulates people with fairly simple goals, it made sense to use a planner to try to string together sequences of actions to achieve them.

We had some concerns about the runtime performance of a planner vis-à-vis the performance goal, so we decided to implement it using a *propositional planner,* due to its potential for very efficient implementation. A detailed description of such a planner is beyond the scope of this short chapter, but we can describe it briefly at a high level. By a propositional planner, we mean one whose pre- and postconditions come from a finite set of grounded propositions, instead of being expressed as predicates. For example, a planning rule in a propositional planner might look like this (using "~" for negation):

```
Rule: Preconditions:  at-home & is-hungry
      Action:         go-to-restaurant
      Postconditions: ~at-home & at-restaurant
```

Compare this with a rule that uses predicate logic, which is more common in planners descended from STRIPS (Fikes and Nilsson 1971):

```
Rule: Preconditions:  (at-location X) &
                      (desired-location Y) & ~(equal X Y)
      Action:         (go-to Y)
      Postconditions: (at-location Y) & ~(at-location X)
```

Predicate rules are more compact than propositional ones—they let us describe relationships between entire families of entities.* At the same time, this expressiveness is

---

* Of course one can also convert predicate rules into propositional rules by doing Cartesian products of the predicates and all the possible values for their free variables, at the cost of exploding the set of propositions.

expensive: The planner has to find not just the right sequence of actions to reach the goal, but also the right set of value bindings for all those free variables.

Propositional rules allow some interesting optimizations, however. Since all propositions are known at compile time, pre- and postcondition can be represented as simple bit vectors—then during planning, the process of checking preconditions and applying postconditions reduces down to very fast bitwise operations. Another benefit is easy plan caching: It is easy to annotate each propositional plan with a bitmask that describes world states in which this plan could be reused, so that it can be cached and reapplied verbatim in the future. At the same time, propositional rules also have a clear shortcoming: they lack the expressiveness of predicate logic, and require more propositions and rules, which complicates the decision of when it makes sense to use them.

Once implemented, the planner's performance exceeded expectations. Although this was early in production and we did not have a full set of NPCs defined yet, we knew intuitively that search space fan-out was not going to be a big issue.* Even so, plan caching was immediately useful: with the relatively small number of NPC types living fairly stereotyped lives, only a handful of distinct plans actually got created and then cached, so the planner only had to run that many times during the course of the game.

We ended up switching away from planning for a reason unrelated to performance, as discussed next. But even so, our takeaways were that (1) we had a positive experience with planning as a way to prototype AI behavior and explore the design space and (2) there are good ways to make it performant enough for use in games (e.g., using propositional planning, or compact GOAP planners such as presented in [Jacopin 2015]).

10.2.2 Second System: Daily Scripts

In the process of implementing character AI, our understanding of our own design changed. We realized that we wanted to have our NPCs live very stereotyped, routinized lives—they should be pretty predictable, because there were too many of them in the building for the player to care about them in detail. We also wanted a lot of designer control over our peoples' daily routines, to enhance the fiction of the game: so that worker and resident behavior would match the socio-economic status of their workplace or apartment, but at the same time, have a lot of variety and quirks for "flavor."

In the end, we realized that *by employing planning, we were working on the wrong level of abstraction.* We were authoring individual planning steps and trying to figure out how to turn them turn into the right behaviors at runtime—but what we actually wanted to do, was to author peoples' *entire daily routines* at a high level, so that we could have strong authorial control over when things happened and how they varied. We needed to author content not on the level of "how am I going to react to this situation," but on the order of "what does my workday look like today, and tomorrow, and the day after tomorrow."

The representation of behavior in terms of *routines* certainly has a rich history in AI. Some of the anthropologically-oriented research (e.g., Schank and Abelson 1977, Suchman 1987), makes a compelling case that our everyday human interactions are

---

* We saw this later re-affirmed by Jacopin in his empirical studies of planning in games (Conway 2015): in many games, NPC planning tends to result in numerous short plans, and relatively small search spaces.

indeed highly routinized: that given standard situations, people learn (or figure out) what to do and when, without having to rederive it from first principles, and these stereotyped routines drive their behavior.

Once we realized we were modeling behavior at the wrong level of abstraction, the solution was clear: we decided to abandon planning altogether, and reimplement NPC behavior as libraries of *stereotyped scripts*, which were descriptions of routine activities such as going to the office, going to a sit-down restaurant and sitting down to eat, processing a repair request from a tenant, and so on. Scripts would then be bundled together into various *daily schedules*, with very simple logic for picking the right script based on current conditions, such as the time of day and the contents of a simple "working memory" (e.g., info on where the NPC wants to go, where its current job is, where its current home is, and so on). Below is an example definition of a daily script, for someone who works long hours at the office:

```
name "schedule-office.7"
blocks [
    { from 8 to 20 tasks [ go-work-at-workstation ] }
    { from 20 to 8 tasks [ go-stay-offsite ] }
]
oneshots [
    { at 8 prob 1 tasks [ go-get-coffee ] }
    { at 12 prob 1 tasks [ go-get-lunch ] }
    { at 15 prob 0.5 tasks [ go-get-coffee ] }
    { at 17.5 prob 0.25 tasks [ go-visit-retail ] }
    { at 20 prob 0.5 tasks [ go-get-dinner ] }
    { at 20 prob 0.25 tasks [ go-get-drink ] }
]
```

This definition is split into two sections. In the blocks section, we see that they work from 8 am to 8 pm at their assigned work station (e.g., their desk), and otherwise spend time at home. Those *continuous* scripts such as go-work-at-workstation are performed as simple looping activity, repetitive but with tunable variations. Then the oneshots section specifies individual *one-shot* scripts that might or might not take place, depending on the probability modifier prob, and each script itself will have additional logic to decide what to do (e.g., go-get-coffee might start up and cause the NPC to go buy a cup of coffee, thus spending money in your building, but if there are no cafes in the building it will abort and cause the NPC to complain). Finally, all of these scripts bottom out in sequences of individual actions, as described in the next section.

This knowledge representation is simple compared to our previous planning approach, but it was a positive trade-off. Interestingly enough, early in preproduction we had also attempted a more complex internal personality models for NPCs, which included physiological state such as hunger or tiredness, but over time we removed all of this detail. The reasons were two-fold: (1) internal state acted as "hidden information" that made it difficult for both the designer and the player to understand why an individual is behaving in a certain way and (2) when multiplied by dozens or hundreds of NPCs, this made for many frustrating moments of trying to understand when entire populations behaved unexpectedly.

Our main take-away was that *the utility of detailed NPC representation is inversely proportional to the number of NPCs the player has to manage*. When the number of simulated people is small, players appreciate them being complex. However, as the number gets larger, this does not scale. Having to understand and manage them in detail becomes a burden for both the player and the designer, so it is better to increase the level of abstraction as the number of NPCs increases, and limit the complexity that the player has to deal with.

10.3 Action Performance

Both of our action selection systems—the planner, and the script scheduler—produced sequences of actions that needed to be performed by the NPC. In this section we will look at the flip side of this coin: action performance. We will also talk about two simplifications that enabled efficient implementation: open-loop action performance, and domain-specific representation for pathfinding.

10.3.1 Action Queues and Open-Loop Action Performance

Many NPC AI systems are *closed-loop feedback systems*—they monitor the world while actions are performed, and adjust behavior appropriately, primarily so that they can handle failures intelligently. This comes at a price, however: checking the world has a nonzero computational cost (based on the frequency of updates, the fidelity of the sensory model, etc.), as does deciding whether to act on this new information. Some architectures like *subsumption* (Brooks 1986) or *teleoreactive trees* (Nilsson 1994) accept constant resensing and recomputation as the cost of doing business—while various *behavior tree* implementations, for example, differ greatly in whether the individual nodes revalidate themselves in teleoreactive fashion or cache their activation for extended periods of time.

In our system we take this to a stark extreme: we run action performance almost entirely *open-loop*, without trying to monitor and fix up our behavior based on changes in the world. The main AI setup looks something like this:

1. Action selection picks a script (e.g., *go to work*), and combines it with the NPC's working memory (e.g., *I work at office #243*) to produce a sequence of simple actions: *go into the lobby, wait for elevator, take elevator, walk into office #243, sit down at my desk, etc.*
2. Actions get dropped into an *action queue* and executed in linear order. This is detailed in (Zubek 2010), but anyone who has played The Sims or classic base-building real-time strategy games will be immediately familiar with how this works at runtime.
3. Each action can optionally monitor for custom failure conditions. For example, a navigation action will fail if a path to the destination cannot be found.
4. If a failure is detected, the queue is flushed immediately, and optionally a fallback script may be queued up instead (e.g., *turn to the camera, play displeased animation, and complain about the conditions in this building*).
5. Once the queue is empty, the system runs action selection all over again, which picks the next set of actions and refills the queue.

In effect the system only evaluates the world when it has nothing to do, and once a course of action is decided, it runs open-loop until it either succeeds or gets interrupted.

These sequences of actions also end up being rather short—for example, a script for going to a restaurant and eating might produce a dozen individual actions, altogether taking about an hour of game time (or: less than a minute of real time) to execute.

This works only thanks to the mostly benign nature of this game world: it is usually okay to run open-loop without paying too much attention to the world. If something unexpected does happen, action selection is so inexpensive that we can just abandon the previous activity and start over. So the brief take-away is that, for game designs that allow it, inexpensive action selection enables a whole host of other simplifications, such as skipping proper failure handling in favor of just starting all over again.

10.3.2 Pathfinding over a Simplified Model

The second optimization had to do with pathfinding. The game takes place on what is essentially a 2D grid—a cut-away side view of a building, which can be, say, 100+ stories tall and several hundred grid cells wide, depending on the scenario. A naive implementation of A* pathfinding on the raw grid representation quickly turned out to be insufficient when hundreds of NPCs tried to navigate the grid at the same time.

Naturally, we reformulated pathfinding to be hierarchical to reduce search space. However, instead of using a generic clustering approach such as for example, HPA* (Botea et al. 2004), we used our domain knowledge to produce a specialized compact representation, which made it easier to support the player making ongoing changes to the path graph (as they built, altered or expanded their highrise). In short: based on the game's design, the pathable space divided up into distinct *floor plates,* which were contiguous sequences of tiles on the same floor, such that the character could do a straight-line movement inside a floor plate. Additionally, each floor plate was connected with those above or below it via stairs, escalators, or elevators, together known as *connectors.* Floor plates and connectors became nodes and edges in our high-level graph, respectively, and movement inside each floor plate became simple straight-line approach.

This search space reduction was significant: for an example of a dense building 100 stories tall by 150 tiles wide with four elevator shafts, we reduced the space from 15,000 grid cells to only 100 graph nodes with 400 edges between them. At this point, the data model was sufficiently small to keep running A*, and additional tweaks to the heuristic function prevented the open set from fanning out unnecessarily.

I should also add that we considered alternatives such as JPS and JPS+ over the raw grid, but found them to be an uneasy fit given that the player would be altering the grid space all the time. In particular, JPS (Harabor and Grastien 2012) effectively builds up a compact representation as needed, in order to simplify its search, but as the player keeps changing the game board it would have to keep redoing it over and over again—which seems less optimal than just keeping the source data model compact to begin with. Additionally, JPS+ (Rabin 2015) gains a performance advantage from preprocessing the search space, but this is an expensive step that is not intended to be reapplied repetitively while the game is running.

In the end, although we considered more complex approaches than A*, they became unnecessary once we realized how to *optimize the search space instead of optimizing the algorithm.* We used our domain knowledge to reduce the data model so drastically that the choice of algorithm no longer mattered, and it was a very positive development. Many areas of AI involve search, and model reduction is a classic technique for making it more tractable.

10.4 Conclusions

Drastic simplifications of character AI allowed us to reach our goal of 1000 NPCs at 60 FPS, while keeping development costs down. It was a good example of the power of a super-specialized AI implementation which, although not generalizable to more complex behaviors or more hostile environments, was an excellent fit to the problem at hand, and carried no extra computational (or authoring) burden beyond the minimum required.

This might be an interesting example of the benefits of tailoring one's AI implementation to fit the problem at hand, instead of relying on more general middleware. Although general solutions have their place, it is amazing what can be achieved by cutting complexity mercilessly until there is nothing left to cut.

References

Botea A., Mueller M., Schaeffer J. 2004. Near optimal hierarchical path-finding. *Journal of Game Development*, 1(1), 7–28.

Brooks, R. 1986. A robust layered control system for a mobile robot. *IEEE Journal of Robotics and Automation*, RA-2(1), 14–23.

Conway, C., Higley, P., Jacopin, E. 2015. Goal-oriented action planning: Ten years old and no fear! *Game Developers Conference 2015*, San Francisco, CA.

Fikes, R. E., Nilsson, N. J. 1971. STRIPS: A new approach to the application of theorem proving to problem solving. *Artificial Intelligence*, 2(3–4), 189–208.

Jacopin, E. 2015. Optimizing practical planning of game AI. In S. Rabin (ed.), *Game AI Pro 2*, CRC Press, Boca Raton, FL.

Harabor, D., Grastien A. 2012. The JPS pathfinding system. In *Proceedings of the Annual Symposium on Combinatorial Search (SoCS)*, Niagara Falls, Ontario, Canada.

Nilsson, N. 1994. Teleo-reactive programs for agent control. *Journal of Artificial Intelligence Research*, 1, 139–158.

Rabin, S. 2015. JPS+: Over 100x faster than A*. *Game Developers Conference 2015*, San Francisco, CA.

Schank, R., Abelson, R. 1977. *Scripts, Plans, Goals, and Understanding*. Lawrence Erlbaum Associates, Hillsdale, NJ.

Suchman, L. 1987. *Plans and Situated Actions*. Cambridge University Press, Cambridge.

Zubek, R. 2010. Needs-based AI. In A. Lake (ed.), *Game Programming Gems 8*, Cengage Learning, Florence, KY.

11 Ambient Interactions
Improving Believability by
Leveraging Rule-Based AI

Hendrik Skubch

11.1 Introduction

It is a hot day in the city of Lestallum. An old man rests comfortably on a bench. Shaded by the nearby palm trees, he reads the local newspaper. A passing tourist takes a break from sightseeing and joins him. Wiping sweat from his forehead, he glances at the newspaper. With a puzzled look in his face, he poses a question to the old man. A brief conversation ensues.

This small scene is one of many that contributes to the realism and vibrancy of a city scenario. Although it is irrelevant for the main plot of a game or for its game play, we value the added immersion. *FINAL FANTASY XV* emphasizes the idea of a journey through a diverse landscape featuring different cultures. In order to bring that world to life and convey different cultures, it is not enough to just place NPCs in the environment. Instead, these NPCs need to interact with the environment and with each other.

This goal leads to two requirements; first, a way to mark up the environment with sufficient information to motivate AI decision-making, and second, a way to express how multiple characters can react to this information. Classical AI scripting methodologies in games such as state machines or behavior trees focus on the actions of individuals. Expressing causal and temporal relationships between the actions of different actors is difficult at best.

We present an interaction-centric approach in which interactions are described using STRIPS-like rules. A type of smart object, called *Smart Locations*, use the resulting scripts to control the actions of multiple NPCs. In contrast to planning, symbolic effects are not used to reason about future world states, but instead are used to coordinate the actions of multiple participants by updating a common knowledge representation in the form of a blackboard and reactively applying rules based on that structure. Thereby coordination becomes the focus of the language and is expressible in a straightforward manner. Moreover, the resulting rule-based scripts are highly adaptive to different situations. For example, in the city scene mentioned above, if there was no old man, the tourist might still sit down to rest. Alternatively, if the old man was joined by a friend, the tourist might have walked by due to lack of space.

11.2 From Smart Objects to Smart Locations

The concept of smart objects was originally conceived for The Sims (Forbus 2002). Smart objects are inanimate objects in a scene that carry information about how they can be used by an agent. For example, a chair may carry the information that it can be used to sit on. It even provides the necessary animation data for doing so. In a sense, by emphasizing objects instead of agents, smart objects reverse the idea of traditional agent-based AI, thereby decoupling the AI from the data necessary to interact with an asset. This allows for new objects to be added to a scene and become usable by the AI without modifications to the AI itself.

More recently, the concept of smart objects has evolved into that of smart zones by de Sevin et al. (2015). Smart zones abstract away from concrete objects and add the idea of roles that NPCs can fulfill, thereby facilitating multiple NPCs interacting with the environment in order to create a richer scene.

In a similar way, smart locations abstract away from concrete objects, as shown in Figure 11.1. They are invisible objects that refer to multiple concrete objects. For example, a single smart location may refer to two chairs and a table. This allows it not only to inform agents about the existence and usability of individual objects, but also to capture relationships between them, such as furniture grouping. Although smart zones use timeline-based scripts with synchronization points to drive the behavior of NPCs, we use a more expressive scripting language based on declarative scripting rules. Furthermore, we add an additional abstraction layer between the location object embedded in the world and the static script object. These script objects may contain additional data necessary for its execution, such as animations. The resulting decoupling allows for scripts to be exchanged, whereas the smart locations stay in place. But smart locations do not just contain information; they essentially govern the usage of the objects they refer to. To that end, they emit signals to agents in the vicinity. These signals can range from mere notifications to commands, depending on the type of emitter. In *FINAL FANTASY XV*, we use four different kinds of emitters:

- *Notification emitter*: These emitters merely inform agents about the existence of the smart location, the objects it knows about, and a set of ontologically grounded tags. Notification emitters are mainly used to inform the more autonomous characters, such as the player's buddies.

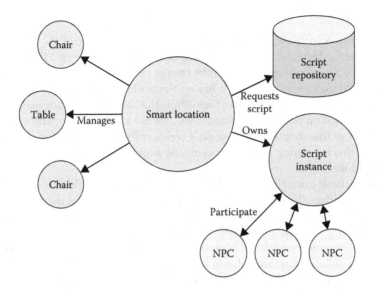

Figure 11.1

Smart locations manage static props and dynamic script instances.

- *Script emitter*: This is the most frequently used emitter type. Based on the number and type of NPCs in the vicinity, this emitter performs a role allocation and initiates the execution of a script. We will elaborate on this process in the following sections.
- *Spawn emitter*: Scripts that require three or more specific characters occur rarely when using just NPCs that pass by the location. This has already been noted by Blondeau during the development of *Assassin's Creed Unity* (Blondeau 2015). Spawn emitters fill this gap by spawning a set of NPCs at points specified by designers. This is also used to place NPCs at otherwise unreachable locations, such as balconies.
- *Player emitter*: Finally, the player emitter communicates with the player by means of interaction icons, which, when reacted to, will initiate a script. The player themselves joins this script as an NPC. Player input is fed to the script's blackboard, allowing designers to script short interactive scenes in a dynamic fashion without changing methodology.

11.3 Expressing Interactive Acts

We express interactions in the form of rule-based scripts. Rules are drawn from STRIPS (Fikes and Nilsson 1971), but instead of being used for planning, they form a declarative scripting language, where rules operate over a special kind of blackboard, a tuple space. Tuple spaces were originally devised as a way to coordinate data access in distributed systems (Carriero et al. 1994). The combination of both methodologies allows agents to exchange information by executing rules on the same tuple space. In the following, we briefly introduce STRIPS and tuple spaces as the two foundations of interaction scripts.

11.3.1 Foundation: STRIPS

Stanford Research Institute Problem Solver, or STRIPS, was one of the first automated planning systems. Here, we refer to the language of that system. In STRIPS, an action is described by a precondition that must be true in order for the action to be executable, and the positive and negative effects it has on the world. Positive effects add facts to the world, whereas negative effects remove them. Note that, although the original formulation of STRIPS is based on pure propositional logic, we use a first-order notation here and in the remainder of this chapter. Since we only consider finite domains under closed-world assumption, this is nothing more than syntactic sugar, as all formulas can be compiled into propositional logic.

Consider a classic example from academia, called the Blocks-world. In this world, a robot is tasked with stacking blocks on a table on top of each other. One of the actions the robot has is $PickUp(B)$—with the intuitive meaning that the robot will pick up a block B with its actuator. The precondition for this action is $onTable(B) \land \neg on(A,B) \land \neg holding(K)$, meaning that B should be on the table, nothing should be on top of it, and the robot should not already be holding anything else in its actuator. The positive effect of this action is $holding(B)$—the robot is now holding block B. The negative effect is $onTable(B)$—the block is no longer on the table. With action descriptions like this, and state descriptions for a goal and an initial state, planning algorithms can chain actions together in order to find a sequence of actions leading from an initial state to a goal state.

Note that the precondition acts as a selector over which block B will be picked up. In Section 11.4.3, we will discuss how both the truth value of the precondition and an assignment for the variables in the rule, such as which block is chosen for variable B, can be determined at the same time by means of a backtracking algorithm.

11.3.2 Foundation: Tuple Space

Tuple spaces are a way to coordinate distributed systems. Since we do not need to operate a truly distributed system, that is, there are no synchronization issues or accidental data loss, we use a simplified version here. The tuple space provides facilities to store, query, and modify facts used in STRIPS rules, such as $onTable(B)$ from above. Basically, a tuple space can be thought of as a multimap, where the name and the arity (arguments) of a predicate (e.g., $onTable/1$) are used as keys to map onto all ground facts currently considered being true. Thus, in this form, it only represents positive knowledge under the closed-world assumption, matching STRIPS and enabling negation as failure reasoning.

11.3.3 The Interaction Language Model

A basic interaction script consists of a set of roles and a set of rules. Intuitively, roles define which kind of actors can participate in a script and how many, whereas rules indicate what the actors are supposed to do.

Whenever an actor is participating in a script, it is assigned exactly one role. Multiple actors can be assigned to the same role. An actor may be able to take on different roles.

For example, the old man on the bench may be able to take on the roles citizen, male, elder, and human, but not waiter or tourist (but in the context of a single script instance, he will take on only one role). More precisely, a role consists of the following:

- *Name*: The unique name of the role, such as tourist, waiter, or citizen.
- *Cardinality*: The minimum and maximum number of actors that can take on this role. Role allocation will try to satisfy all cardinalities of the script. If that is not possible, the script will not start. Should any cardinality be violated while the script is running, for example because an actor left, the script will terminate.
- *Flags*: An extensible set of flags that further describes how a role is to be treated at runtime. Most importantly these flags govern whether or not an actor can dynamically take on a role and join the script while it is running, or if any special actions are necessary when an actor is leaving the script, such as sending them a command to move away from the smart location.

We may describe the initial scene between the old man and the tourist with these roles:

- *Elder*: 0..1 dynamicJoin = true
- *Tourist*: 0..2 dynamicJoin = true

Thereby, the script can run with any combination of up to two tourists and one elder. Any role initially unfulfilled can be assigned later dynamically. This permits a variety of different sequences of events; for example, the old man may join the tourist on the bench.

In contrast to roles, rules entail what actors should do once they participate in a script. In a minimal version of this scripting language, rules must consist of at least:

- *Precondition*: The condition that has to hold in order for the rule to fire.
- *Action*: The action an actor should undertake. Note that actions are optional; rules without actions simply apply their effects and can be used to chain more complex effects. In our case, each action identifies a state machine or behavior tree on the lower individual AI level. The degree of abstraction is arbitrary, but we think a reasonable degree is achieved by actions such as "sit down," "go to," or "talk to." Of course, this depends on the concrete game considered.
- *Action parameters*: A list of key-value pairs that are passed to the lower layer that executes the action. For example, movement speed or animation variations often occur as parameters.
- *Addition* (δ^+) *and Deletion* (δ^-): The list of positive and negative effects a rule has. They are applied immediately when the rule fires.
- *Deferred Addition and Deferred Deletion*: Similar to Addition and Deletion, the deferred versions modify the tuple space. However, they are applied only after the action has successfully terminated. If there is no associated action, deferred effects are applied immediately.
- *Termination type*: A rule can be used to terminate the whole script or cause an individual actor to leave the script. The termination type is used to indicate this.

Additionally, we added the following syntactic sugar to simplify common cases:

- *Target*: Most actions have a target, as is implied by the proposition in their name such as goto or lookat. Because these are used so frequently, we treat the target separately instead of using action parameters.
- *Role*: Acting as an additional precondition, the role property of a rule limits the NPCs that can execute a rule to those of the corresponding role.
- *State*: A state also acts as an additional precondition. Only actors currently inhabiting this state can execute this rule. Thereby we overlay the rule-based execution with a simple state machine. It is trivial to formulate state machines using preconditions and action effects; however, a simple state machine greatly reduces the perceived complexity and length of preconditions.
- *Next state*: After successfully executing a rule, an NPC will transition to this state.
- *OnError*: In order to simplify handling of errors stemming from failed actions, a list of facts can be provided to be added if a rule fails.

Treating these notions explicitly simplifies the task of writing scripts, and, in many cases, allows optimizing script execution further. For example, by rearranging rules so that rules of the same state are consecutive in memory, only rules of the current state of an actor have to be evaluated.

Let us consider some simple example rules useful for the bench scenario. First, we need a rule for sitting down:

- **Rule 1**:
    - **Action:** $\text{sit}(X)$
    - **Precondition:** $\text{seat}(X) \wedge \neg\text{reserved}(X, Y)$
    - δ^+: $\text{reserved}(X, .me)$
    - **deferred** δ^+: $\text{sitting}(.me) \wedge \text{timer}(.me, .now + randf(2, 5)^* .minute)$

The action sit has a target, namely the object to sit on, denoted by the variable X, which is sent as a game object to the individual AI. The implementation of sit may be arbitrarily complex, in this case, it will query the animation system for where to be in relation to X when triggering the sit-down animation, path plan to that point, move, and finally trigger the animation.

The specific game objects that X can possibly refer to at runtime are known by the smart location. Before executing the script, the smart location dumps this information into the tuple space using the predicate seat. The second predicate, reserved, is used to formulate a reservation system inside the tuple space. Note that the keyword reserved does not have any meaning outside of the rule for sitting. The definition of the rule gives meaning to the symbol. The same holds true for the predicates sitting and timer which are used to inform other NPCs that the sitting action has now been completed and to store a timer for future use, respectively. The difference between addition and deferred addition allows us to reserve the seat the moment the action is committed to, while informing other NPCs of the action completion several seconds later.

However, not everything can be solved purely by means of the tuple space, sometimes we need to call into other systems or refer to special purpose symbols. These symbols are

11. Ambient Interactions

prefixed with a dot "." as in $.me$, which refers to the NPC that is currently evaluating the rule. Therefore, the positive effect reserved$(X, .me)$ will substitute X with the game object that represents the seat and $.me$ with the NPC in question before inserting the resulting tuple into the blackboard. Once the NPCs are sitting, we can drive a simple randomized sequence of talking and listening actions using the following three rules:

- **Rule 2:**
  - **Precondition:** $\neg\text{talker}(X) \land .any(Y) \land \text{sitting}(Y)$
  - δ^+: $\text{talker}(Y)$

- **Rule 3:**
  - **Action:** $\text{talk}(X)$
  - **Precondition:** $\text{talker}(.me) \land .any(X) \land X \neq .me \land \text{sitting}(X)$
  - **Deferred δ^-:** $\text{talker}(.me)$

- **Rule 4:**
  - **Action:** $\text{listen}(X)$
  - **Precondition:** $\text{talker}(X) \land X \neq .me$

Rule 2 does not cause an action; it is merely used to designate a single sitting NPC as the currently talking one by means of the predicate talker. The built-in predicate $.any$ unifies its argument with a random participating NPC. The following predicate sitting limits this to a random sitting NPC. The backtracking algorithm achieving this behavior will be discussed in Section 11.4.3.

Rule 3 triggers a talk-action for the designated NPC. Supplying another random sitting NPC as target X, allows for LookAt-IK and other directed animations to take place. After the talk-action finishes, talker is removed, in turn triggering the first rule again. The fourth rule lets us model a listening reaction to the talking action, such as a nod.

Finally, in order to avoid an endless discussion between the NPCs, we add a termination rule that refers to the timestamp introduced in Rule 1, which causes the NPCs to get up and terminate its participation in the script:

- **Rule 5:**
  - **Action:** getup
  - **Precondition:** $\text{timer}(.me, T) \land T < .now$
  - **Terminate = true**
  - δ^-: $\text{timer}(.me, T)\ \text{sitting}(.me)$
  - **Deferred δ^-:** $\text{reserved}(.me, X)$

Note the free variable X in the deferred deletion causes all matching tuples to be removed from the tuple space.

Formally, our query language is limited to conjunctions of literals. A literal is a possibly negated predicate such as reserved(X, Y) or $\neg$talker(Z). Thus, we exclude disjunctions and negations over the scope of multiple literals from the language. Furthermore, the query language also relates to DataLog (Ceri et al. 1989), a function-free declarative language.

That means function symbols are not allowed to occur, thereby greatly reducing the complexity of evaluation compared to other declarative languages, such as Prolog. We can still tolerate function symbols to occur by simply enforcing them to be evaluated immediately when they are encountered, circumventing any costly term manipulation. This allows us to express functional terms such as $.now + randf(2,5) * .minute$ in Rule 1, or $distance(.me, Someone)$ without incurring the cost of term manipulation in a full first-order language. A tool side verification step ensures that this treatment of function symbols is safe, for example, that $Someone$ will always be instantiated to an NPC when evaluating $distance(.me, Someone)$.

11.4 Script Execution

A smart location equipped with a script emitter will periodically query a spatial database for NPCs in the vicinity in order to start an interaction scene. Based on the smart location's preference for different scripts, the NPCs found, and the currently loaded scripts, a script is chosen to be executed. From there on, the script is updated regularly in the following way:

- Shuffle all participants. This counters any unintentional bias in the rule set toward the first or last NPC. Any predicate that accesses participants effectively accesses the shuffled list.
- Apply the deferred effect of any action that finished and the OnError list of any failed action.
- For each participant not currently executing an action, find the first matching rule in its state. If found, trigger the action and apply the effect.
- Remove all NPCs from the script that encountered a termination flag.
- Terminate the script if not enough NPCs remain.

Since scripts operate on a local blackboard, each NPC only participates in at most one script at a time, and smart locations have exclusive ownership over their props, multiple script instances can be executed concurrently without the need for thread synchronization.

11.4.1 Role Allocation

Role allocation is the process of assigning actors to roles such that the resulting assignment satisfies all given constraints, such as our cardinalities. In practice, we use additional constraints to reflect that some NPCs, such as families, act as groups and only join scripts together. Since each actor can satisfy multiple roles and each role may require multiple actors, the problem is NP-hard (Gerkey and Mataric 2004). However, the specific problem instances encountered in interaction scripts are typically very small and simple, meaning rarely more than three or four distinct roles and rarely more than five actors. Furthermore, we do not require the resulting allocation to be optimal with respect to some fitness function. Indeed, we can even allow the role allocation to fail occasionally. Thus we can formulate role allocation as a Monte-Carlo algorithm by randomizing its input.

After randomization, role allocation simply assigns NPCs greedily to roles until the lower bound of the respective cardinality is reached. If a role-cardinality cannot be satisfied in this way, the allocation fails immediately. Subsequently, potentially remaining NPCs are assigned until the maximum cardinality is reached or no more NPCs can be added.

11.4.2 Joining Late

Although a smart location is running a script, it will not start a second one to avoid concurrent access to its resources. However, it will periodically query the spatial data base for NPCs in the vicinity that can join the already running script instance. Whether or not this is possible is indicated by the flag "dynamicJoin" introduced in Section 11.3.3. This behavior allows for more dynamic scenes where NPCs come and go, such as street vendors serving pedestrians walking by.

11.4.3 Rule Evaluation

At its core, our rule-based scripting language is declarative in nature. This means that execution and evaluation are often the same. For example, successfully evaluating a precondition will result in an assignment of values to its variables. Rule evaluation is based on two main algorithms: unification and backtracking search.

Unification is an essential algorithm for term manipulation. Given two terms, unification decides whether or not they can be equal and, if so, applies an equalizing substitution. For example, the term 2*X+f(A, B) can be unified with 2*A+K by substituting X with A and K with f(A, B). For details, consult work on automated reasoning, such as done by Fitting (Fitting 1996).

Since we draw from DataLog and evaluate function symbols immediately, we can simplify unification to three cases: constant to constant, variable to constant, and variable to variable. The first case becomes a simple equality check, and is the only case that can fail. The second case is a pure assignment, and only the last case requires a more work, as the system has to keep track of which variables are unified with each other. We recommend to identify variables with indices and, for each variable, to keep track of the respective variable with the lowest index it has been unified with.

The second algorithm needed, backtracking, is a common method to search for a solution in a structured space, such as a conjunction of literals. Its origins are lost in history, the earliest known application of this algorithm was done by Ariadne to solve Minos' labyrinth (cf. Morford et al. 2013). In essence backtracking explores the state space by successively expanding options and returning to earlier states if it encounters a failure or if it exhausts all options at a particular junction.

Hence, backtracking requires the ability to reestablish a former state in the space explored. In general, this can be achieved with three different techniques: saving the previously visited states, recomputing them from the start, or undoing actions applied. We use a combination of the first two options; we save whatever was assigned to the variables of the rule in the previously visited state, but require any predicate to compute its nth solution from scratch without saving data leading to solution $n-1$. Alternative solutions using scratchpad stack memory are possible, but have not been explored in the context of this work. For further reading on backtracking algorithm we recommend literature discussing DPLL algorithms for SAT solving (Davis et al. 1962), such as (Nieuwenhuis et al. 2004).

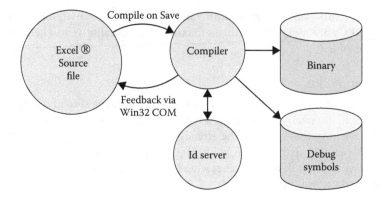

Figure 11.2

The build chain transforms textual scripts into an interpretable binary format.

11.5 Build Chain

The success of any novel scripting methodology depends on its ease of use. We designed the build chain, as shown in Figure 11.2, to provide quick iteration cycles and make use of tools designers are typically familiar with. Scripts are edited in Excel, where table oriented perspective lends itself well to rule-based scripting. Upon saving, a compiler translates the XML source to a binary loadable by the runtime. All identifiers used in the script, such as roles, predicates, and actions are translated to unique 32-bit identifiers by means of an id-server. In order to supply a debug UI with readable names again, a separate file with debug symbols is generated.

11.5.1 Validation

The mathematically grounded properties of STRIPS allow us to detect various scripting errors during compilation and supply feedback directly into the editor. Most notably, we can detect common problems such as:

- Unreachable states.
- Unexecutable rules (specialization of rules of higher precedence).
- Usage of uninstantiated variables.

However, the Turing completeness of the scripting language prevents us from detecting all problems.

11.6 Extensions

The concepts presented here were used heavily during production of *FINAL FANTASY XV*. Naturally, we made adjustments to the original system to accommodate unforeseen needs and situations.

- *Beyond agents*: Although actions of NPCs are easily representable in the language presented, achieving other effects, such as opening a shop UI or reacting to the player clicking an icon was not. Most of these issues relate to the communication with other game systems. We addressed this by wrapping these systems into proxy objects that participate in a script as if they were NPCs. Thus the shop itself becomes an NPC with available actions such as opening and closing specific shop pages. Moreover, these proxy objects push information about ongoing events in their domain into the blackboard. For example, the shop informs the script of what the player is buying or selling. The shopkeeper's reaction can then simply be driven using the blackboard.
- *Templating*: During development, we discovered sets of highly similar scripts being used throughout the game, such as scripts controlling different shopkeepers. The logic within the scripts was almost identical, but various parameters such as motion-sets and shop configurations were changed. We countered this effect by allowing for one script to include another as a base and introduced meta-parameters that the script compiler would replace before creating the binary. Thus we introduced a string templating system in the tool chain. The runtime was completely agnostic about this since it only sees the resulting scripts.

11.7 Conclusion

In this chapter, we presented a novel way of scripting interactions between ambient NPCs using STRIPS rules that modify a blackboard shared by participating NPCs. We described how the necessary information to ground a script in its environment can be supplied by situated objects, namely smart locations, which govern the usage of multiple props. Furthermore, we presented the relevant algorithms for evaluation and role allocation. This approach shifts the modeling focus from the actions of the individual to the interaction between multiple agents and thus significantly simplifies the representation of multiagent scenes encountered in living breathing city scenarios.

The declarative nature of the rule-based approach caused an initially steep learning curve for our designers, but was adopted after a brief transition period. Compared to other scripting methodologies, three advantages became apparent during the development cycle:

- *Locality*: Problems are contained within a single script and thus easier to find.
- *Adaptability*: Scripts adapt themselves naturally to a wide variety of situations.
- *Validation*: The ability of the script compiler to find common mistakes early on greatly reduced iteration time.

References

Blondeau, C. Postmortem: Developing systemic crowd events on Assassin's creed unity, GDC 2015.

Carriero, N. J., D. Gelernter, T. G. Mattson, and A. H. Sherman. The Linda alternative to message-passing systems. *Parallel Computing*, 20(4): 633–655, 1994.

Ceri, S., G. Gottlob, and L. Tanca. What you always wanted to know about datalog (and never dared to ask). *IEEE Transactions on Knowledge & Data Engineering*, 1(1): 146–166, 1989.

Davis, M., G. Logemann, and D. Loveland. A machine program for theorem proving. *Communications of the ACM*, 5(7): 394–397, 1962.

de Sevin, E., C. Chopinaud, and C. Mars. Smart zones to create the ambience of life. In *Game AI Pro 2*, ed. S. Rabin. Boca Raton, FL: CRC Press, pp. 89–100, 2015.

Fikes, R. E. and N. J. Nilsson. Strips: A new approach to the application of theorem proving to problem solving. Technical report, AI Center, SRI International, Menlo Park, CA, May 1971.

Fitting, M. *First-order Logic and Automated Theorem Proving* (2nd Ed.). Springer-Verlag New York, Inc., Secaucus, NJ, 1996.

Forbus, K. Simulation and modeling: Under the hood of The Sims, 2002. http://www.cs.northwestern.edu/~forbus/c95-gd/lectures/The_Sims_Under_the_Hood_files/v3_document.htm (accessed July 5, 2016).

Gerkey, B. P, and M. J. Mataric. A formal analysis and taxonomy of task allocation in multi-robot systems. *The International Journal of Robotic Research*, 23(9): 939–954, 2004.

Morford, M., R. J. Lenardon, and M. Sam. *Classical Mythology* (10th Ed.). Oxford University Press, New York, 2013.

Nieuwenhuis, R., A. Oliveras, and C. Tinelly. Abstract DPLL and abstract DPLL modulo theories, *Proceedings of the International Conference on Logic for Programming, Artificial Intelligence, and Reasoning*. Montevideo, Uruguay: LPAR, pp. 36–50, 2004.

12

Stochastic Grammars
Not Just for Words!

Mike Lewis

12.1 Introduction

Randomness, when carefully and judiciously applied, can be a powerful tool for augmenting the behavior of game AI agents and systems. Of course, purely random behavior is rarely compelling, which is why having some semblance of pattern is important. One way to do this is to simulate *intent*, making AI decisions based on some kind of deliberate design. Many excellent resources exist for creating the illusion of intentional behavior in game AI—and this very volume is not least among them.

However, there are times when it is useful to tap directly into the realm of randomness. Even if it is purely for the sake of variety, a little bit of random fuzz can do a lot of good for an AI character (Rabin et al. 2014). Occasionally, though, there is a sort of confluence of requirements that makes both purely intentional decision-making and heavily randomized decision-making problematic. It is at those times that *structured randomness* comes into play.

Imagine a mechanism for generating sequences of actions. This mechanism can be tuned and adjusted, either at design-time, or on-the-fly at runtime. It creates a controlled blend between predictable patterns and random chaos. That is to say, the mechanism can be tweaked to create arbitrarily "random-feeling" sequences based on completely customizable factors. Again, this can be done statically or dynamically. Moreover, it can generate any kind of structured data. Sound appealing?

Welcome to the world of *stochastic grammars*.

12.2 Formal Grammars

A *formal grammar* is a tool for describing and potentially manipulating a sequence or stream of data. Ordinarily, grammars are used for textual inputs, and operate on sequences known as *strings*. Although historically envisioned by Pāṇini, circa the 4th century BCE, as a tool for rewriting sequences, grammars are also instrumental in recognizing whether or not a string is *valid* according to the rules of the grammar itself (Hunter 1881).

This recognition of validity, along with *parsing*—extracting syntactic structure from a string—is a key component in both natural language processing and computer languages. A compiler, for example, typically uses a tool called a *parser generator* to convert a grammar into code that can parse strings written by those grammatical rules—that is, programs (Brooker et al. 1963).

As an example, Table 12.1 shows a simple grammar that describes the natural numbers.

This grammar uses Extended Backus-Naur Form, or EBNF (Backus 1959, Wirth 1977). Each row of the table describes a *rule*. The third rule, "Natural Number," can be thought of as the starting point for recognizing or generating a natural number. It specifies a *sequence* of symbols, beginning with a nonzero digit. The comma indicates that the following portion of the rule is concatenated with the leading portion. Next, the braces indicate *repetition*. In this case, any digit may appear, and that sub-rule is allowed to apply zero or more times.

Looking at the actual rule for nonzero digits, there is one additional important symbol, the pipe. This indicates *alternations*, that is, that a choice must be made from several alternatives. Each rule also ends in a semicolon, denoting the termination of the rule.

The net result is that the "Natural Number" rule specifies a nonzero digit followed by any number of digits (including zeros). This matches perfectly with the expectation for what a natural number looks like.

However, grammars need not be relegated to use with pure text or numbers. If a string is defined as a set of data *symbols* with some particular set of meanings, virtually any structured data can be defined with a suitable grammar. Allowing these symbols to carry meanings like "punch" or "attack on the left flank" opens the door for much richer applications than mere operations on words.

Table 12.1 Grammar Describing the Natural Numbers in EBNF

Name of Rule	Rule Matches Strings of this Form
Nonzero Digit	1|2|3|4|5|6|7|8|9;
Any Digit	Nonzero Digit|0;
Natural Number	Nonzero Digit, {Any Digit};

12.3 Generating Sequences from a Grammar

Grammars typically have a selected set of *starting symbols* which control the first rule(s) used when creating a new string. How does one choose which rules of a grammar to follow in order to generate a sequence? If the goal is to exhaustively generate as many strings as possible, then the answer is simply "all of them." Sadly, this is not useful for most non-trivial grammars, because they are likely to contain recursive rules that just never stop expanding.

Suppose that each rule of the grammar is augmented with a weight value. As the output is progressively accumulated, there will (probably) be points where more than one rule from the grammar can be applied. In these cases, the next rule can be chosen via a simple weighted random number generation, using the weights from each available rule. This structure is known as a *stochastic grammar* or *probabilistic grammar*.

Supplementing a grammar with this random selection process is akin to describing how "likely" a given generated string might be. If a sequence describes actions taken by an AI agent, the probability weights control that agent's "personality." Some actions—and even subsequences of actions—can be modeled as more "like" or "unlike" that character, and in this way, a sort of preferential action generation process can be constructed.

Take, for example, a ghost wandering a *Pac-Man*-like maze. At each intersection, the ghost can turn left, turn right, continue forward, or reverse directions. Table 12.2 illustrates a simple grammar that describes these possibilities; note the addition of weights to the Direction Decision rule's alternation pattern.

The ghost AI simply needs to generate a string of decisions and pop a decision from the front of the queue each time it enters an intersection. If an "L" decision is retrieved, the ghost turns left; correspondingly, the ghost turns right for an "R." The "F" decision translates to moving forward in the same direction as before, and "B" indicates moving backward. Obviously in some cases a particular decision may not be applicable, so the ghost can simply pop decisions until one is possible. Should the queue become empty, just generate a new sequence and continue as before.

As described in the table, the stochastic grammar will have an equal chance of making each possible selection. However, the "personality" of the ghost can be adjusted to bias toward (or against) any of the options available, merely by tuning the weights of the grammar.

What other sorts of things can be done with a decision-making grammar? Consider a raid boss in a multiplayer RPG. This boss has two basic attack spells: one that makes enemies in a small region vulnerable to being set on fire, and a separate fireball which capitalizes on this vulnerability. Moreover, the boss has a third, more powerful spell that does huge bonus damage to any foe who is currently ablaze.

The naïve approach is to simply cast the vulnerability spell on as many players as possible, then fireball them, and lastly close with the finishing move. Although this is a workable design, it lacks character and can easily be predicted and countered by attentive players.

Table 12.2 Stochastic Grammar to Control a Ghost in a Maze

Name of Rule	Rule Generates these Symbols
Direction Decision	0.25 L|0.25 R|0.25 F|0.25 B;
Navigation Route	{Direction Decision};

Table 12.3 Grammar Producing Attack Sequences for a Raid Boss

Name of Rule	Rule Matches Strings of This Form
Vulnerability Combo	Vulnerability, {Fireball};
Basic Sequence	Fireball, {Vulnerability Combo}, Finisher;
Attack Sequence	{Fireball}, {Basic Sequence};

Instead, describe the available moves for the boss in the form of a grammar, such as that in Table 12.3. One possible sequence generated by this grammar might look like "Fireball × 3, Vulnerability × 5, Fireball × 4, Finisher, Fireball, Finisher." More importantly, given appropriate probability weights for the rules, this grammar will produce different sequences each time the raid is attempted. Although the overall *mechanics* of the fight are intact, the *specifics* vary wildly. That is to say, players know they must come equipped to defend against fire, but the actual progression of the fight is largely unpredictable.

Although arguably the same results could be had with a more sophisticated AI system, it is hard to compete with the raw simplicity and easy configurability of a stochastic grammar. Certainly, there will be applications for which grammars are not the best choice. However, when used appropriately, the ability to generate a structured, semi-random sequence is a compelling tool to have in one's arsenal.

12.4 A Data Structure for Grammars

The actual implementation of code for generating (and parsing) strings is a rich subject. However, it is quite possible to work with simple grammars using basic, naïve approaches to both parsing and generation. Given a suitable data structure for representing the grammar itself, it is easy to start with the trivial implementation and upgrade to more sophisticated algorithms as needed.

Based on the examples so far, some kind of tree-type structure seems well suited to the task of representing the grammar itself. Each rule can be represented as a node in the tree. A "nested" rule can be pointed to as a child node. The nodes themselves can contain a list of parts, with each part being either a sequence of nodes or a list of weighted alternatives to choose from. Within this structure, nodes can be represented using an abstract base class, with derivative classes for sequences and alternations. The actual generated sequence (or input for parsing) can be represented with a container class such as std::vector or equivalent. Each node should have an interface function for generating (or parsing) the substrings for which it is responsible.

Leaf nodes are the simplest case; they will merely append an element to the sequence and return. These nodes represent the *terminals* of the grammar. Next up, sequencer nodes contain a set of node pointers. When they are asked to generate an element, these nodes traverse the container of child nodes in order, asking each one to recursively generate an element. This process can optionally be repeated randomly, so that the sequence itself appears some random number of times in the final output, in keeping with the rules of the grammar.

Alternations, or choices, are where the magic of a stochastic grammar really happens. These nodes store a set of child nodes, like before, but this time each child has an associated weight value. As the node is traversed, *one* child node is selected to be traversed recursively, based on a weighted random selection from the available children. (See the accompanying demo code at http://www.gameaipro.com/ for an example implementation.)

12.5 Streaming Sequences

The approach to generation thus far has focused on creating a finite-length sequence, using random weights to control the length and content of each generated string. However, it can sometimes be useful to generate *infinitely long* sequences as well.

Superficially, this might be denoted by setting a sequence node's weight such that it never chooses to stop repeating. However, there is more to the problem—with the methods described so far, generating an infinite sequence in this way will just exhaust available memory and fail to return anything.

There are two basic approaches to "streaming" an infinite sequence based on a generative grammar. On the more sophisticated side, one might allow *any* sequence node to be infinite, regardless of its position in the grammar/tree. This requires some careful gymnastics to preserve the state of a pass when the output is retrieved midway through.

A hackier alternative is to simply allow only the root node to be infinite. Instead of configuring it as a truly infinitely-repeating node, however, it should be wired up to run exactly once. Then, the grammar simply invokes the root node some random number of times in order to generate a "window" into the current sequence. The resulting output is buffered and can be consumed at any arbitrary rate. Conceptually, the sequence behaves as if it were infinitely long, but the process of generating new subsequences is easily accomplished in finite time.

It should be pointed out that grammars are hardly the only tool for generating such infinite sequences. In fact, if the characteristics of the sequence are *context sensitive*, that is, the upcoming output depends on the value of previous output; an approach like *n*-grams is probably much more useful (Vasquez 2014).

12.6 Grammars as Analogues to Behavior Trees

When considering the design and application of a stochastic grammar, it can be helpful to think of them as limited behavior trees (Isla 2005). As seen earlier, a grammar can often be represented as a tree (although a directed graph is needed in the case where rules form cycles). Each rule in the tree can be thought of as a node in a behavior tree, by loose analogy.

Sequences and alternations map directly to sequence and selection nodes in BTs. The primary distinction is that, for a stochastic grammar, the logic for choosing how to proceed is not based on examining game state, but simply rolling a random number. So a stochastic grammar provides a tool for mimicking more complex AI decisions using a weighted random behavioral pattern rather than something more intentional.

The process for designing a stochastic grammar can closely parallel the process of designing a simple behavior tree. Clearly, the stochastic grammar will make far less deliberate and reactive actions in general, but with careful weight tuning, a fuzzy behavior model can look remarkably similar to a more intentional model.

Choosing to use a grammar over a BT is primarily a matter of considering two factors. First, if the behavior tree is designed to carefully handle contingencies or special cases of world state, it is probably not suitable for replacement with a grammar. Second, the design of the agent being controlled may lend itself to a more randomized behavioral pattern, in which case grammars are an excellent choice. A simple way to recognize this is to check for heavy use of random selector nodes in the behavior tree.

One last potential benefit of the grammar model is that it is cheap to evaluate, since it does not require many world state queries and can operate purely on a stream of random numbers. This makes grammars an excellent tool for simulating large numbers of agents with low-fidelity "intelligence."

12.7 Grammars as Scripting Engine

One of the more powerful ways of looking at grammars is as a tool for generating tiny scripts. If the generated symbols are miniature commands for a scripting engine, grammars define the rules by which those commands can be combined into meaningful programs. Working with this analogy, the goal is to first specify a set of commands that are useful for handling a given AI problem, and then specify a grammar that will produce effective sequences of those commands.

The advantage of using a grammar to generate such script programs is that the scripts themselves need not be static. New scripts can be created on-the-fly as gameplay unfolds. Since the rules for creating a script are defined during the game's implementation, any generated script has a reasonable chance of doing the "right thing"—assuming the rules are suitably constrained.

One way of looking at this is that grammars are a key part of dynamically reprogramming a game's behavior as it is played. As long as a given grammar is well-designed, it will produce new behavioral scripts that are effective within the game simulation itself. Controlling the weights of rules in the grammar yields the power to adjust the "success rate" of any given script on-the-fly. Clearly, the possibilities for this are endless.

Generally speaking, any time an AI system (or other game system!) expresses behavior in terms of sequences of actions, a grammar can be deployed in place of handcrafted scripts. Moreover, given the relationship between grammars and *deterministic finite automatons*, it is possible for any behavior generated by a finite-state machine to also be expressed by a grammar (Zhang and Qian 2013).

There is clearly ample material in a typical game's AI—and, again, other game systems—that could be supplanted by the crafty use of grammars. Grammar-like methods known as *Lindenmayer-systems* (or *L-systems*) are already in popular use for procedural generation of certain kinds of geometry, ranging from trees and rivers to buildings and even entire cities (Rozenberg and Salomaa 1992). Some creative users of L-systems have even explored creating gameplay mechanics based on the technique (Fornander 2013).

12.8 Tuning a Stochastic Grammar

One of the classic methods for computing appropriate weights for a stochastic grammar given a preexisting corpus of sequences is the *inside-outside algorithm* (Baker 1979). This approach computes probabilities of various strings appearing in a given grammar, starting from an initial estimate of each probability. It can then be iteratively applied until a training string's probability reaches some desired point. Indeed, if a corpus of training data is available, this method is the definitive starting point for tuning a grammar.

But what if training data is not available? The primary difficulty of tuning the grammar then becomes generating enough sample outputs to know whether or not the overall distribution of outputs is desirable. Strictly speaking, most stochastic grammar approaches use a *normalized probability* of each rule being selected in the output generation process. This is mathematically elegant but can make it difficult to estimate the overall traits of the grammar, since the human mind is notoriously bad at probabilistic reasoning.

As a compromise, the accompanying demo code does not adhere to a strictly normalized probability model for all of the rules. Some shortcuts have been taken to simplify the tuning process. Namely, *subsequences* have a probability of repeating, which is independently applied after each successful generation of that subsequence. If the random roll fails, the subsequence ends. Further, *alternations* (selections from among several options) employ a simple weighted random scheme to allow the grammar creator to control the relative "importance" of each option.

Although not strictly compliant with the preexisting work on the subject of stochastic grammars, this approach is arguably far simpler to reason about intuitively. More importantly, the tuning process is as simple as generating a large number of outputs, and hand-editing the weights and probabilities of various elements of the grammar to suit.

On an opinionated note, the transparency of the modified stochastic grammar concept is tremendously important. Although probabilistic grammars are typically viewed as a machine learning technique, they need not provoke the negative reaction to machine learning that is so common in game AI circles—because they do not inherently carry the need to give up fine-grained control and intuitive results. Compared with other approaches, the lack of explicit training can actually be a huge boon, since it eschews the "black box" nature of many other learning tools. Designers can rest assured that the grammar will produce *comprehensible* if not directly predictable results.

Moreover, it is trivial to dynamically exploit the direct relationship between weights in a stochastic grammar and the frequency of output patterns. If a grammar produces too many occurrences of some subsequence, the weight for that sequence can simply be decreased at runtime. Of course, the tricky part here is attaching sufficient metadata to the final sequence such that the rules responsible for a particular excessive subsequence can be identified easily. This flexibility (and transparency) is far more cumbersome to build into a system like an artificial neural network or a genetic algorithm.

12.9 Feeding a Grammar with Utility Theory

Another approach to generating weights for a stochastic grammar is to measure them using *utility theory* (Graham 2014). In this technique, the weight of a given node is computed through a scoring mechanism that evaluates how "useful" that node is in a given context. For instance, suppose a turn-based strategy AI has three basic options: attack, reinforce defenses, or expand to new territory. This AI can be given a stochastic grammar for deciding its moves for the next several turns.

Table 12.4 Stochastic Grammar Decides How a Strategic AI Plays the Game

Name of Rule	Rule Generates these Symbols
Smart Turn	0.4 Attack|0.3 Reinforce|0.3 Expand;
Offensive	Attack, Attack, {Smart Turn};
Turtling	{Reinforce}, {Smart Turn};
Conquest	Attack, Expand, {Smart Turn}, Expand;

When moves are needed, the AI recalibrates the weights of each option based on evaluating the current battlefield. Depending on the grammar it uses, the AI can express various "personality" differences. Consider the example grammar in Table 12.4.

In this model, the AI has three basic personalities to choose from. The Offensive personality will attack two times followed by a series of "smart" choices based on utility. AIs that prefer to "turtle" will reinforce their defenses for an arbitrary period, then make a few "smart" moves. Lastly, expansionistic AIs will attack and expand heavily, sprinkling in a few "smart" turns as well.

The default calibration for "smart" moves has Attack turns slightly preferred to Reinforce and Expand selections—but imagine if the AI could calculate *new* weights for these options on-the-fly. If the utility score for a particular move is exceptionally high, that strategy will dominate the AI's play for several turns. Conversely, if the utility score is low, the AI is less likely to favor that selection.

Ultimately, the result is that AIs will tend to play according to a particular style, but also mix things up periodically with sensible moves based on situational reasoning. A moderate style could even be used which simply does the "smart" thing all the time. More sophisticated play styles can be constructed with almost arbitrary power and flexibility, just by expanding the grammar.

12.10 Conclusion

Stochastic grammars are a widely used tool from natural language processing. They have seen limited use outside that field, despite being applicable to a number of interesting problems, when applied creatively.

By generating sequences of data in a controlled—but still random—fashion, stochastic grammars enable the creation of highly structured—but not perfectly predictable—outputs. Such outputs can be suitable for many game AI and game logic tasks, ranging from design-time procedural content creation to actual on-the-fly behavior controllers.

Although slightly unorthodox in the realm of game AI, grammars offer a much higher degree of designer control than many other machine learning techniques. As such, they are a promising tool for the inclusion in every game AI professional's toolbox.

For those interested in further research, the author highly recommends (Collins).

References

Backus, J. W. 1959. The syntax and semantics of the proposed international algebraic language of the Zurich ACM-GAMM Conference. *Proceedings of the International Conference on Information Processing, UNESCO.* 125–132.

Baker, J. K. 1979. Trainable grammars for speech recognition. *Proceedings of the Spring Conference of the Acoustical Society of America.* 547–550.

Brooker, R.A.; MacCallum, I. R.; Morris, D.; Rohl, J. S. 1963. The compiler-compiler. *Annual Review in Automatic Programming* 3:229–275.

Collins, M. Probabilistic Context-Free Grammars http://www.cs.columbia.edu/~mcollins/courses/nlp2011/notes/pcfgs.pdf (accessed July 10, 2016).

Fornander, Per. 2013. *Game Mechanics Integrated with a Lindenmayer System.* Bachelor's Thesis, Blekinge Institute of Technology. http://www.diva-portal.se/smash/get/diva2:832913/FULLTEXT01.pdf (accessed July 10, 2016).

Graham, Rez. 2014. An introduction to utility theory. In *Game AI Pro,* ed. S. Rabin. Boca Raton, FL: CRC Press, pp. 113–126.

Hunter, Sir William Wilson. 1881. *Imperial Gazetteer of India.* Oxford: Clarendon Press.

Isla, Damian. 2005. *Managing Complexity in the Halo 2 AI System.* Lecture, Game Developers Conference 2005. http://gdcvault.com/play/1020270/Managing-Complexity-in-the-Halo (accessed July 10, 2016).

Rabin, Steve; Goldblatt, Jay; and Silva, Fernando. 2014. Advanced Randomness Techniques for Game AI: Gaussian Randomness, Filtered Randomness, and Perlin Noise. In *Game AI Pro*, ed. S. Rabin. Boca Raton, FL: CRC Press, pp. 29–43.

Rozenberg, Grzegorz; Salomaa, A, eds. 1992. *Lindenmayer Systems: Impacts on Theoretical Computer Science, Computer Graphics, and Developmental Biology.* Verlag/Berlin/Heidelberg: Springer.

Vasquez, Joseph II. 2014. Implementing N-Grams for player prediction, procedural generation, and stylized AI. In *Game AI Pro,* ed. S. Rabin. Boca Raton, FL: CRC Press, pp. 567–580.

Wirth, Niklaus. 1977. What can we do about the unnecessary diversity of notation for syntactic definitions? *Communications of the ACM*, Vol. 20, Issue 11. 822–823.

Zhang, Jielan; and Qian, Zhongsheng. 2013. The equivalent conversion between regular grammar and finite automata. *Journal of Software Engineering and Applications*, 6:33–37.

13

Simulating Character Knowledge Phenomena in *Talk of the Town*

James Ryan and Michael Mateas

13.1 Introduction

There are many examples of stealth and action games that use complicated knowledge, perception, and alertness models to produce short-term NPC beliefs that are a core part of gameplay (Diller et al. 2004, Welsh 2013, Walsh 2015)—here, notable examples include *Thief: The Dark Project* (Leonard 2003), *Fable* (Russell 2006), and *Third Eye Crime* (Isla 2013). Few projects, however, have supported characters whose perceptual systems instantiate memories or lasting beliefs, and there are even fewer examples of the modeling of *fallible* character memory (Ryan 15). Meanwhile, issues of belief—especially false belief—are often central in other fictional media (Palmer 2004). Some games *are* about character beliefs, to be fair, but in these cases beliefs are typically handcrafted, as in *LA Noire* (Team Bondi 2011). In games that do model character knowledge procedurally, the AI architecture that handles such concerns is often called a *gossip system* (Crawford 2004). A classic example of this type of architecture drives the reputation system in *Neverwinter Nights* (BioWare 2002), whereas more recent examples include the rumors system of *Dwarf Fortress* (Adams 2015, Ryan 15) and the beliefs system of Versu (Evans and Short 2014). Frequently, however, gossip systems in games provide only ancillary support to core gameplay. As such, we find that games that are about character beliefs model them with human-authored scripts, whereas games that model such knowledge procedurally tend to do so secondarily to core gameplay.

In this chapter, we present an architecture that, to our knowledge, simulates character knowledge phenomena more deeply than any earlier system has (Ryan 15), all in service of a game that is fundamentally about character beliefs, called *Talk of the Town*.*

Although the game is still in development, the architecture that we present in this chapter is fully implemented. Relative to other gossip systems, like the ones in *Neverwinter Nights* and *Dwarf Fortress*, our system takes a fiercely agent-driven approach, with character knowledge propagating as a result of discrete character interactions. This contrasts the more typical method of abstractly modeling information flow across the gameworld. While the latter approach is more computationally efficient, it would undermine a number of our goals for the *Talk of the Town* player experience, as we discuss in depth at the end of this chapter.

13.2 *Talk of the Town*

Talk of the Town is an asymmetric multiplayer *dwarflike* (a game in the mold of *Dwarf Fortress* [Adams 2015]) that features character knowledge propagation as a core mechanic. In this section, we describe its story, simulation, and our gameplay design; the simulation is fully implemented, but the gameplay layer is currently being developed.

13.2.1 Story

The story that frames gameplay surrounds the death of a very important person in the town in which gameplay takes place. This person had accumulated considerable wealth and produced several descendants who now constitute an aristocracy in the town. Many of these family members had been anticipating the person's death for the inevitably large inheritances that would thereby be disbursed, but in his or her last moments the person apparently signed a document willing everything to a secret lover whose existence had not been known to the family. In one week, the town will gather at a theater to remember the deceased and to witness the reading of his or her will, but the family plans to ascertain the identity of the lover and apprehend this person before the document can ever be delivered to the presiding attorney. Meanwhile, the town is abuzz with rumors about the mysterious lover, whom a handful of witnesses briefly observed on the night of the death.

13.2.2 World Generation

Prior to gameplay, the town is simulated from its founding in 1839, when a handful of families converge on an empty townscape to establish farms, through the death of the central character in the summer of 1979. As in *Dwarf Fortress*, this *world generation* procedure causes a number of structures that are critical to gameplay to emerge bottom-up from the simulation itself. Specifically, these are the town's physical layout (namely the locations of its businesses and homes), its residents' daily routines, and, most importantly, the town's social and family networks that knowledge propagates over. Elsewhere, we provide a detailed account of how character social networks, in particular, are produced (Ryan 16c). Throughout this

---

* The development of *Talk of the Town* is being carried out by a growing team comprising James Ryan, Michael Mateas, Noah Wardrip-Fruin, Adam Summerville, Tyler Brothers, Tim Hong, Joyce Scalettar, and Jill Yeung. Adam Summerville also contributed to the design of the architecture described in this section.

simulation procedure, NPCs act out daily routines across day and night cycles by either going to work, going on errands, dropping by places of leisure, visiting friends and family, or staying at home. Additionally, characters may, for instance, start a business, hire an employee, build a house, marry another character, give birth to a new character, and so forth. NPCs decide what to do by utility-based action selection (Mark 2009). When at the same location (a home or business), characters may interact at probabilities that depend on their relationship and their personalities. From a simple affinity system, continued interaction may breed contempt, friendliness, or romantic feelings (these work unidirectionally and may be asymmetric) (Ryan 16c). The combinatorics of these simple character behaviors over more than a century of game time is enough to generate rich social, family, and work networks by the time that gameplay takes place, at which point around 300–500 NPCs will live in the town.

13.2.3 Gameplay

Talk of the Town's gameplay layer is still being implemented, so in this section we will describe its design. The game is multiplayer and asymmetric: one player, the *lover*, controls the lover character and the other player, the *family member*, controls a member of the deceased person's family. The lover's goal is to go undetected until the will ceremony, while the family member works to ascertain the lover's appearance before that time.*

Gameplay culminates in a scene showing the town's citizens filing into the theater for the will ceremony, during which time the family member must select the person who best matches his or her conception of the lover—if this player selects correctly, he or she wins; otherwise, the lover wins.

The town is represented as an isometric, tile-based 2D world, spanning nine-by-nine city blocks. Each tile contains either part of a street, part of a building (home or business), or part of an empty lot. Players navigate their characters across the town by moving across tiles using directional inputs. When a building is close, the player can click on it to have his or her character enter it. Building interiors are also rendered as tile-based 2D environments, with tiles containing furniture and characters. When an NPC is close enough to the player character, the player can click on him or her to engage in conversation. This is *Talk of the Town*'s core gameplay interaction, since it is how the player will solicit and spread information. Additionally, player characters can patronize certain businesses through dialog interaction with employees—this is critically how the lover can change his or her character's appearance (e.g., getting a haircut at a barbershop or buying glasses at an optometrist).

We are ambitiously aiming for dialog interaction in *Talk of the Town* that is fully procedural, extending our earlier work on *Façade* (Mateas and Stern 2004). Conversations will proceed by turns, with NPCs producing generated dialog and players typing in their dialog in free text. We have already developed a fully implemented *dialog manager*, which is a module that handles conversation flow, updates NPC beliefs according to the semantic content of utterances, and reasons about conversational norms to form content requests on behalf of NPCs (Ryan 16a). Content requests are then processed by a *natural language generation* (NLG) module, which produces NPC dialog on-the-fly; this system is also fully

---

* A given character's appearance is the composite of 24 facial attributes—for example, hair color, hair length, eye color, and nose size—that are inherited from the character's parents.

implemented, with a prototype that allows NPCs to engage in small talk using a pool of nearly three million generable lines of dialog (Ryan 16d).

For *natural language understanding* (NLU)—the task of processing arbitrary player utterances into semantic representations—we are in the early stages of developing an approach that uses deep neural networks (Summerville et al. 2016). NLU is a notoriously difficult challenge, and so we have contingency plans for another dialog-system design in the event that our method does not work well enough; this interface would enable players to construct modular utterances out of dialog components, somewhat in the style of Chris Crawford's Deikto language (Crawford 2007) or *Captain Blood*'s UPCOM interface (Exxos 1988). In any event, deployed utterances will be displayed as speech bubbles emitting from the characters who speak them. By virtue of our dialog manager and NLG module, NPCs may engage in background conversation with one another. If the speech bubbles they emit are in view, the player can eavesdrop on the conversation; we plan to use this both as a storytelling device and a way of improving the believability of background characters (Ryan 16e).

Gameplay will proceed by day and night timesteps that span the week leading up to the will ceremony, with players taking a turn on each timestep. We hope for gameplay to be networked, but we have contingency plans involving local multiplayer and AI opponents. Player turns will be constrained either by a time limit or by a notion of resources (to be spent on a combination of navigation steps, conversation turns, and elapsed time). Between turns, character knowledge phenomena are simulated (see next section), crucially allowing for the propagation of information originating in the player activity of the last turn.

As their character is well-established in the town, the strategy of the family member will be characterized by *management* of the town's knowledge network. This is because the dialog manager reasons about how NPCs will respond (including whether to divulge information) by considering their affinities toward their interlocutors (Ryan 16c). Being quite established in the town, the family member is more likely to encounter NPCs who are comfortable being open with him or her. As such, this player will likely spend his or her turns soliciting town residents for gossip about the lover (whose mysterious identity is the titular *Talk of the Town*). Here, both apparently true and apparently false information are useful. True information obviously helps the family member to ascertain the lover's identity, but patently false information could have actually originated with the lover—a fundamental family-member strategy thus becomes homing in on the sources of apparently deliberate misinformation.

The lover's strategy, then, is to *pollute* the town's knowledge network by changing his or her character's appearance and spreading misinformation about the identity of the mysterious lover (through dialog interaction with NPCs). Given the above, however, it is critical for this player to not pollute the network too extravagantly, because this could lead the family member right to the lover character's identity. One core lover tactic will be using *false flags*, that is, intelligently claiming other characters as the original sources of any misinformation that he or she attempts to spread. We also want the lover to be able to reason about whom exactly to impart misinformation to. As NPCs are more open to characters they know and like, this will promote tactics that require the lover to build up trust relationships with NPCs, so that they will be more likely to believe and propagate misinformation. As noted above, gameplay ends with the town filing into the theater for the will ceremony, at which point the family member must attempt to select the lover from a lineup by clicking on the character that best matches his or her conception of that person.

Broadly, we want the gameworld to feel like it is sprawling with rich NPCs who each have their own unique experiences that are captured by the particular beliefs that they have adopted. In this way, we hope that navigating the town and interacting with NPCs will feel like exploration, but with the depth of the gameworld being expressed more in its character belief structures than in its modest physical size.

13.3 Simulating Character Knowledge Phenomena

Characters in *Talk of the Town* build up knowledge about the world as they go about their daily routines. In this section, we describe our simulation of character knowledge phenomena, including the mechanisms by which knowledge may originate, propagate, deteriorate, and terminate according to the procedures of our architecture.

13.3.1 Overview

People and places in the gameworld have perceptible features, which characters may directly observe to form beliefs about them. Such knowledge may then propagate across characters during social interactions. Critically, character knowledge may also be misremembered (in multiple interesting ways), or be altogether forgotten. All throughout, the system keeps track of belief histories and knowledge trajectories, because we anticipate visualizing summaries of this kind of information at the end of gameplay.

13.3.2 Requirements

Our method has some architectural requirements, which we will list in this section. First, characters must have *perceptible attributes*, meaning attributes that are directly observable by other characters. In *Talk of the Town*, these are mainly physical features, like hair color, but we also model *conditionally* perceptible attributes—for instance, a character's workplace is observable while they are in the act of working.

Next, a *radius of perceptibility* must be modeled, where characters within the radius of another character may observe his or her perceptible attributes. This radius is also used to determine whether a nearby character is close enough to eavesdrop on a conversation, as we will discuss later. As we model space discretely in *Talk of the Town*, we simply say that characters at the same location in town are near enough to perceive one another.

Additionally, system authors must craft a procedure for determining *character saliences*. Character saliences work together with attribute saliences, described next, to determine the probability of knowledge phenomena occurring for a given character and attribute—that is, the probability of a perceptible attribute being observed, as well as the probability of a belief about any attribute being propagated, misremembered, or forgotten. In Section 13.3.6, we explain salience computation in more depth.

Similarly, our architecture uses specified *attribute saliences*, which prescribe how likely given character features are to be observed and to be talked about among characters. In *Talk of the Town*, this specifies, for instance, that a person's hair color is more salient than the shape of her chin.

Finally, authors must also produce a *belief mutation graph*, which specifies how particular character beliefs can mutate, and at what probabilities. We discuss belief mutation in more detail in Section 13.3.8, and Figure 13.3 shows excerpts from the belief mutation graph authored for *Talk of the Town*.

13.3.3 Ontological Structure

As illustrated in Figure 13.1, a character's composite knowledge of the world is structured as an *ontology* of interlinked mental models that each pertain to a single person or place. The interlinking occurs when a character's belief about some attribute of a character or place resolves to some other character or place for whom or which they have another mental model. For instance, a character may believe that a person works at some business in town, and so his or her belief about that person's workplace would itself link to his or her mental model of that business. We use this ontological structure for elegance and convenience, because it allows characters to reason about entities in terms of knowledge they may already have about related entities (rather than by instantiating redundant or potentially inconsistent knowledge). In the case of a character knowing where another character works, this allows the former to reason about, for example, the character's work address in terms of existing knowledge about that place that can be stored and accessed independently of knowledge about the character who works there.

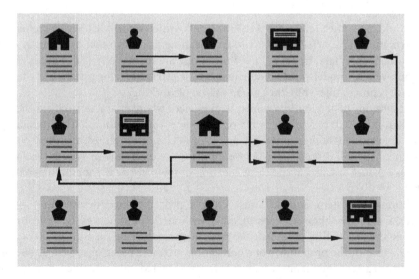

Figure 13.1

An illustration of the *ontological* structure of character knowledge: characters build up mental models of the hundreds of people, homes, and businesses in their towns, each of which might include pointers to other mental models (e.g., a belief about a character's workplace will resolve to a pointer to the mental model for that business).

13.3.4 Mental Models

Characters in *Talk of the Town* form *mental models* about the residents and places in their towns. Each character mental model pertains to a specific individual entity and is structured as a list of *belief facets* that correspond to individual attributes of that entity. A given character attribute will have a *type* (e.g., hair color) and a ground-truth value (e.g., `brown`), but a belief facet corresponding to it will represent a character's potentially false belief about that attribute (e.g., `black`). The attribute types that we have implemented for *Talk of the Town* match the domain and central concerns of the game and are as follows:

- For mental models of characters:
  - *Status*: Condition (`alive` or `dead`), year of departure from the town (if any; e.g., `1972`), marital status (`single`, `married`, `divorced`, or `widowed`).
  - *Age*: Birth year (e.g., `1941`), death year (if any), approximate age (e.g., `30s`).
  - *Name*: First name, middle name, last name, suffix, surname ethnicity (e.g., `German`), whether surname is hyphenated.
  - *Appearance*: Each of the 24 facial attributes that we model (e.g., hair color).
  - *Occupation*: Company (links to mental model of that place), job title (e.g., `bartender`), shift (`day` or `night`), status (`retired`, `employed`, or `unemployed`).
  - *Home*: Home (either an apartment unit or house; links to mental model of that place).
  - *Whereabouts*: Where a person was on a given day or night (links to mental model of that place). This facet is central to the *Talk of the Town* game design, because the lover character is known to have been at the home of the central character on the night of the death.
- For mental models of businesses/homes:
  - *Employees/residents*: Listing of its employees/residents (each links to mental model of a character).
  - *Apartment*: Whether it is an apartment unit (for homes only).
  - *Block*: For example, `800 block of Lake Street`.
  - *Address*: For instance, `613 Fillmore Street`.

We would like to emphasize that these example facet types are only meant to serve as examples, as our method is agnostic to the type of knowledge that it is used to represent. Each facet is structured as a collection of data about the belief. In addition to its *owner* (the character who has constructed the mental model), *subject* (the entity to whom it pertains), and facet type, these data include:

- *Value:* A representation of the belief itself, for example, the string `brown` for a belief facet pertaining to hair color, or the integer `1944` for a facet corresponding to a character's birth year.
- *Mental model:* If the value of this facet resolves to another entity for whom the owner of this facet has formed a mental model, this will point to that mental model. This is how the linking that we have mentioned in earlier examples is handled.

- *Predecessor*: The belief facet that the owner previously held, if any. This allows the system to track supplanted or forgotten character knowledge. As a given chain of predecessors represents a perfect history of an NPC's beliefs about some attribute, we do not plan to give NPCs access to these data.
- *Parents*: If this knowledge originated in information from other characters, this will point to the belief facets of those characters that spawned this current facet. This allows the system to trace the history and trajectory of any piece of information.
- *Evidence*: A list of the pieces of evidence by which the owner of this facet formed and continues to substantiate it; evidence may accumulate as the simulation proceeds. In Section 13.3.5, we outline our evidence typology.
- *Strength*: The strength of this particular belief. This is the sum of the strength of all pieces of evidence supporting it, the determination of which we also explain in Section 13.3.5.
- *Accuracy*: Whether or not the belief is accurate (with regard to the *current* true state of the world).

13.3.5 Evidence

All character knowledge is formed in response to evidence, and may also propagate, deteriorate, or terminate in ways that can be described using pieces of evidence. We will illustrate these details by explaining our evidence typology, which comprises eleven *types* across five categories. This is the most important part of this chapter.

- How knowledge originates:
  - *Reflection*: A reflection represents the case of a character inherently knowing something about himself or herself. We do not spend any computation on actually simulating this phenomenon.
  - *Observation*: When a character directly observes a person or place, he or she may form knowledge about attributes of that entity. Whether knowledge is formed about a particular attribute depends on the salience of the entity and the attribute type, which we explain in Section 13.3.6.
  - *Transference*: If one entity reminds a character of another entity (determined by feature overlap between his or her respective mental models of them), he or she may unconsciously copy beliefs about one to the mental model of the other.
  - *Confabulation*: By confabulation, a character *unintentionally* concocts new knowledge about some entity; this happens probabilistically. The particular belief-facet value that gets confabulated is determined probabilistically according to the distribution of that feature type in the town. For instance, if 45% of characters in the town have black hair, then confabulation of a belief about hair color would have a 45% chance of producing the value black.
  - *Lie*: A lie occurs when an NPC *intentionally* conveys information to another character that he or she himself or herself does not believe. We call this a type of origination (and not propagation) because the knowledge in question is *invented* by virtue of the lie—that is, no existing knowledge is propagated by the lie.

- *Implant*: For efficiency reasons, some essential character knowledge will be directly implanted in character minds at the end of world generation, and thus will have no explicit point of origination. We discuss knowledge implantation in depth in Section 13.3.10.
- How knowledge reinforces itself:
  - *Declaration*: Whenever a character delivers a statement, the strength of his or her own belief (being declared by the statement) will slightly increase. That is, the more a person retells some belief, the stronger that belief becomes for him or her, which is realistic (Wilson et al. 1985). By this mechanic, an NPC who frequently tells the same lie might come to actually believe it.
- How knowledge deteriorates:
  - *Mutation*: As an operationalization of memory fallibility, knowledge may mutate over time. We explain this more thoroughly in Section 13.3.8.
- How knowledge terminates:
  - *Forgetting*: To further incorporate memory fallibility, knowledge may be forgotten due to time passing; this is affected by a character's memory attribute and the salience of the facet subject and type.

Characters are not consciously aware of transferences, confabulations, or mutations, and recipients (and eavesdroppers) of lies treat them as statements. That is, the recipient will reason about a lie as if it were a statement (and so the strength of a lie, as a piece of evidence, is equal to that of a statement), but the system will still track that it was in fact a lie, to allow for the presentation of true knowledge trajectories after gameplay. Additionally, each piece of evidence has metadata of the following types:

- *Source*: With a statement, lie, or eavesdropping, this specifies the character who delivered the information. This allows the system to trace the history and trajectory of any piece of information, which is a design goal.
- *Location*: Where the piece of evidence originated (e.g., where an observation or statement took place).
- *Time*: The timestep from when a piece of evidence originated (either a day or night of a particular date).
- *Strength*: The strength of a piece of evidence is a floating-point value that is determined by its type (e.g., a statement is weaker than an observation) and decays as time passes. In the case of statements, lies, and eavesdroppings, the strength of a piece of evidence is also affected by the affinity its owner has for its source and the strength of that source's own belief at the time of propagation.

13.3.6 Salience Computation

When a character observes some entity in the simulation, a procedure is enacted that determines, for each perceptible attribute of the observed entity (as defined in Section 13.3.2), the probability that the character will remember what he or she saw; this procedure crucially depends on the *salience* of the entity and attribute being observed. Salience computation in *Talk of the Town* considers the relationship of an observed character (subject) to the observer (e.g., a coworker is more salient than a stranger), the extent of the observer's friendship with the subject, the strength of the observer's romantic feelings toward the subject, and finally the subject's job level (characters with more elevated job positions are treated as more salient). For places, salience computation currently considers only whether the observing character lives or works at the observed place. Additionally, our salience–computation procedures consult a hand-authored knowledgebase specifying attribute saliences—this was one of the requirements listed in Section 13.3.2. Salience is also used to determine the probability that a character will misremember or altogether forget (on some later timestep) knowledge pertaining to a given subject and attribute—here, the probability of memory deterioration decreases as these saliences grow larger.

13.3.7 Knowledge Propagation

The salience of the subject and attribute type of a piece of information also affects whether a character will pass it on (via a statement, defined in Section 13.3.5). Currently, what subjects of conversation come up in an interaction between two *conversants* is determined by the salience of all entities that either of them knows about (i.e., the sum salience to both conversants). The n highest-scoring[*] entities are then brought up in conversation, with n being determined by the strength of the conversants' relationship and also their respective *extroversion* personality components. This is illustrated in Figure 13.2. For each subject of conversation, the conversants will exchange information about individual attributes of that subject at probabilities determined by the salience of each attribute type. As a character may bring up subjects that an interlocutor does not (yet) know about, our propagation mechanism allows characters to learn about other people and places that they have never encountered themselves. It is even possible for a character to learn about another character who died before he or she was

Figure 13.2

An illustration of the procedure by which NPCs decide whom to exchange information about. A pair of conversants score everyone they know about for their saliences to both of them, and then select the n highest scoring (where n is determined by the characters' relationship and personalities) to be the subjects of their knowledge exchange.

---

[*] For greater efficiency, we amortize this computation by keeping track of all pairwise character salience scores as relevant changes to the social state occur.

13. Simulating Character Knowledge Phenomena in *Talk of the Town*

born; this often occurs when parents tell their children about deceased relatives (who score highly in salience computation due to being related to both conversants).

13.3.8 Fallibility Modeling

As an operationalization of memory fallibility, characters may adopt false beliefs for reasons other than lies. On each timestep after world generation, the four phenomena associated with memory fallibility—transference, confabulation, mutation, and forgetting (see Section 13.3.5)—are probabilistically triggered for character mental models. When this happens, the facets of that mental model are targeted for deterioration at probabilities determined by the character's memory attribute (modeled as a floating-point value inherited from a parent), the facet type (e.g., a whereabouts belief will be more likely to mutate than a first name belief), and the strength of the existing belief (weaker beliefs are more likely to deteriorate). For mutation, the system relies on a handcrafted schema that specifies for a given facet value, the probabilities of it mutating to each other's viable facet value. Figure 13.3 shows excerpts from this schema, which we call a *belief mutation graph*; earlier, in Section 13.3.2, we noted the specification of this graph as an architectural requirement.

13.3.9 Belief Revision

Currently, an NPC will always adopt a new belief on encountering a first piece of evidence supporting it, assuming there is no current belief that it would replace. As a character accumulates further evidence supporting his or her belief, its strength will increase commensurately to the strength of the new evidence. As noted in Section 13.3.5, the strength of a piece of evidence depends on its type; if the evidence has a source, its strength will also depend on the affinity that its recipient has for that character and the strength of the corresponding belief held by the source.

If at any time an NPC encounters new evidence that contradicts his or her currently held belief (i.e., supports a different belief-facet value), the character will consider the strength of the new evidence relative to the strength of his or her current belief. If the new evidence is stronger, he or she will adopt the new belief that it supports; if it is weaker, he or she will *not* adopt a new belief, but will still keep track of

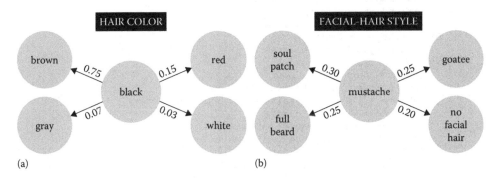

(a)   (b)

Figure 13.3

Illustrative excerpts from our hand-authored *belief mutation graph*. Probabilities specify how particular beliefs about hair color (a) and facial-hair style (b) might mutate (to model character misremembering).

the other *candidate belief* and the evidence for it that he or she had encountered. If he or she continues to encounter evidence supporting the candidate belief, he or she will update its strength accordingly and if at any time that strength exceeds the strength of the currently held belief, the NPC will adopt the candidate belief and relegate the previously held belief to candidate status. Belief oscillation is possible, as such, but that is an appeal of the design. For an example illustrating how this procedure works, see our earlier paper on the system (Ryan 15).

13.3.10 Knowledge Implantation

In our architecture, procedures related to character knowledge phenomena are expensive. If we enacted them during *world generation*—the period of game time that is simulated prior to gameplay and spans from the town's founding in 1839 up to 1979 (see Section 13.2.2)—we would spend a lot of computation simulating the knowledge of hundreds of characters who would have died long before the period of gameplay. Instead, world generation employs all aspects of the simulation *besides* the ones related to character knowledge (e.g., characters forming relationships, starting businesses) and then terminates one week prior to the death of the central character (the event that kicks off gameplay, as explained in Section 13.2.1). At this point, however, living characters have no knowledge at all—to resolve this, the system employs a procedure that *implants* into each character's mind the knowledge that would believably be ingrained in them. This procedure is illustrated in Listing 13.1.

Listing 13.1. Pseudocode for our *knowledge implantation* procedure, which is carried out at the end of world generation.

```
for resident of town
    implants = []
    for immediate family member of resident
        add immediate family member to implants
    for friend of resident
        add friend to implants
    for neighbor of resident
        add neighbor to implants
    for coworker of resident
        add coworker to implants
    for every other character who has ever lived
        chance = 1.0 - (1.0/salience of that character)
        if random number < chance
            add other character to implants
    for character in implants
        for attribute of character
            chance = attribute salience
            chance += -1.0/salience of that character
            if random number < chance
                have resident adopt accurate belief for attribute
```

13.3.11 Core Procedure

After implanting character knowledge, we simulate all character activity, including all knowledge phenomena, for one week of game time (up to the death of the central character). Listing 13.2 shows the operation of this method, with a focus on knowledge-related activity. A variant of the loop is also carried out during gameplay, between player turns.

Listing 13.2. High-level pseudocode for the core procedure of our simulation of character knowledge phenomena.

```
do world generation // See Section 13.2.2
do belief implantation // See Listing 13.1
while central character still alive // One week of game time
    advance one timestep
    for resident in town
        enact resident routine // Put somewhere in the town
    for resident in town
        for nearby character at same place as resident
            if characters will interact // See Section 13.2.2
                do knowledge exchange // See Section 13.3.7
    for resident in town
        do simulation of fallibility phenomena // See Section 13.3.8
```

13.3.12 Tunable Parameters

Our approach has many parameters that can be tuned for both authorial control and greater computational efficiency. In our implementation, belief mutation is quite expensive, in part because we represent many facet values as strings. Although this aspect of our implementation is currently efficient enough for our needs, it presents a basic opportunity for optimization. Beyond this, mutation rates could simply be turned down (as a way of targeting either greater efficiency or gameworlds with more accurate character beliefs). Other tunable parameters include the salience of characters and attributes; the probabilities of social interactions, eavesdropping, lying, and different kinds of knowledge deterioration; the base strengths of each type of evidence; and more. We currently do have worries about the complexity of interaction between all these parameters; eventually, we may end up simplifying some of these systems.

13.3.13 Some Statistics

A typical *Talk of the Town* will be inhabited by between 300–500 NPCs, each of which will maintain approximately 250–400 mental models; some highly extroverted characters will have as many as 500–600 mental models. Across all his or her mental models, a typical character will own around 800–1200 belief facets by the time gameplay begins. The entire world-generation procedure lasts (on the order of) a few minutes, and the simulation of knowledge phenomena between turns takes about a minute; we expect these durations to decrease as we begin to explore optimization strategies closer to release.

13.4 Discussion

Talk of the Town gameplay would not be possible without the architecture we have presented here. First, as we stated above, a fundamental goal of ours is to provide a gameworld that feels like it is sprawling with rich NPCs who each have unique subjective experiences that are captured by the particular beliefs that they have adopted. If we were to model information flow abstractly, as other gossip systems have done, we would lose all this depth and complexity. Further, we want dialog with NPCs to be a core gameplay interaction—with a coarser, more abstract representation of character knowledge, there would not be much for characters to say. Beyond supporting our intended gameplay esthetic, our architecture critically enables the kind of player strategies that we want to support, which were also detailed above.

First, we want the family-member player to be able to home in on the identity of the lover by investigating apparent sources of deliberate misinformation. This requires information flow to be modeled at a considerable level of fidelity, and it also necessitates the possibility of misinformation propagating from specific sources at specific times. Further, we want the lover to be able to tactfully spread *some* amount of information without making his or her identity obvious, but hitting this sweet spot could be tough with coarser-grained modeling of information flow.

With our approach, we are more confident about signals of deliberate misinformation being readable to both players, because knowledge propagation is modeled at the agent level; intuitively, this fidelity of simulation is more likely to match player expectations than abstract models. Still, we want it to be possible for the lover to be successful at clandestinely propagating misinformation—this requires that benign misinformation also be present in the gameworld, which our architecture supports through its simulation of memory fallibility. Moreover, we wish to support a specific tactic that may underpin the lover's larger strategy of spreading misinformation: the ability to propagate *false flag* sources for his or her own misinformation, meaning characters whom he or she claims told his or her what are in fact his or her own lies. False flags are easily represented in our architecture as metadata attached to discrete character beliefs—namely the *source*, *location*, and *time* attributes of pieces of evidence supporting an NPC's belief—that can be surfaced in generated dialog, for example, *Gary Stuart told me last night at the 3rd Street Diner*.

As our game is still in development, we cannot speak conclusively yet about the success of our architecture from an authorial standpoint. One potentially huge challenge that we anticipate involves balancing the architecture's considerable array of tunable parameters—attribute saliences, mutation rates, and so on. Although *Talk of the Town* is not fully implemented yet, we have actually already used this framework in an award-winning mixed-reality experience called *Bad News* (www.badnewsgame.com, Ryan 16b). Over the course of performing this piece more than one hundred times, we have encountered thousands and thousands of generated character beliefs. Although these beliefs have generally appeared to be well-formed and believable, in early performances we noticed a prevalence of misremembered home addresses, including cases where characters could not remember where their own parents lived. To fix this, we simply turned down the mutation rate for this attribute, which seemed to be a good preliminary indication of the prospects for authorial control in the face of so many tunable parameters. As another fundamental limitation, our method is not very computationally efficient, though in Section 13.3.12 we named a few opportunities for optimization. For *Talk of the Town*, we are not particularly worried about this, because the heavy computation takes place prior to gameplay (generating the town) and between player turns (simulating knowledge phenomena).

It is not easy for us to articulate how this architecture could be utilized for games in mainstream genres. We do think there are probably viable opportunities for this (at least in cases where computational efficiency is not a major concern), but we are more excited about fundamentally new kinds of gameplay experiences that could be made possible by our architecture. Here, we hope that *Talk of the Town*, once completed, will do well to demonstrate the appeal of gameplay surrounding the character knowledge phenomena whose simulation we have described in this chapter.

Acknowledgments

We thank Damián Isla for invaluable feedback that greatly improved this chapter.

References

Adams, T., 2015, Simulation principles from Dwarf Fortress. In *Game AI Pro 2: Collected Wisdom of Game AI Professionals*, ed. S. Rabin. Boca Raton, FL: CRC Press, pp. 519–522.

BioWare, 2002, *Neverwinter Nights*. New York: Infogrames/Atari.

Crawford, C., 2004, *Chris Crawford on Interactive Storytelling*. Berkeley, CA: New Riders Press.

Crawford, C., 2007, Deikto: A language for interactive storytelling. In *Second Person: Role-Playing and Story in Games and Playable Media*, ed. P. Harrigan and N. Wardrip-Fruin. Cambridge, MA: MIT Press.

Diller, D.E., W. Ferguson, A.M. Leung, B. Benyo, and D. Foley, 2004, Behavior modeling in commercial games. *Behavior Representation in Modeling and Simulation*.

Evans, R. and E. Short, 2014, Versu—A simulationist storytelling system. *IEEE Transactions on Computational Intelligence and AI in Games* 6(2):113–130.

Exxos (ERE Informatique), 1988, *Captain Blood*. Lyon: Infogrames.

Isla, D., 2013, Third eye crime: Building a stealth game around occupancy maps. In *Proceedings of the 9th Annual AAAI Conference on Artificial Intelligence and Interactive Digital Entertainment*, October 14–18, 2013, Boston, MA: Northeastern University.

Leonard, T., 2003, Building an AI sensory system: Examining the design of thief: The dark project. *Game Developers Conference*, March 4–8, 2003, San Jose, CA: San Jose Convention Center.

Mark, D., 2009, *Behavioral Mathematics for Game AI*. Boston, MA: Cengage Learning PTR.

Mateas, M. and A. Stern, 2004, Natural language understanding in Façade: Surface-text processing. In *Proceedings of the 2nd International Conference on Technologies for Interactive Digital Storytelling and Entertainment*, June 24–26, 2004, Darmstadt, Germany: Computer Graphics Center.

Palmer, A., 2004, *Fictional Minds*. Lincoln: University of Nebraska Press.

Russell, A., 2006, Opinion Systems, *AI Game Programming Wisdom 3*, Cengage Learning.

[Ryan 15] Ryan, J.O., A. Summerville, M. Mateas, and N. Wardrip-Fruin, 2016, Toward characters who observe, tell, misremember, and lie. In *Proceedings of the 2nd Workshop on Experimental AI in Games*, November 14–15, 2015, Santa Cruz, CA: University of California.

[Ryan 16a] Ryan, J., M. Mateas, and N. Wardrip-Fruin, 2016, A lightweight videogame dialogue manager. In *Proceedings of the 1st Joint International Conference of DiGRA and FDG*, August 1–6, 2016, Dundee, Scotland, UK: Abertay University.

[Ryan 16b] Ryan, J.O., A.J. Summerville, and B. Samuel, 2016, Bad News: A game of death and communication. In *Proceedings of the 2016 CHI Conference Extended Abstracts on Human Factors in Computing Systems*, May 7–12, 2016, San Jose, CA: San Jose Convention Center.

[Ryan 16c] Ryan, J., M. Mateas, and N. Wardrip-Fruin, 2016, A simple method for evolving large character social networks. In *Proceedings of the 5th Workshop on Social Believability in Games*, August 1, 2016, Dundee, Scotland, UK: Abertay University.

[Ryan 16d] Ryan, J., M. Mateas, and N. Wardrip-Fruin, 2016, Characters who speak their minds: Dialogue generation in Talk of the Town. In *Proceedings of the 12th Annual AAAI Conference on Artificial Intelligence and Interactive Digital Entertainment*, October 8–12, 2016, Burlingame, CA: Embassy Suites by Hilton San Francisco Airport - Waterfront.

[Ryan 16e] Ryan, J., M. Mateas, and N. Wardrip-Fruin, 2016, Generative character conversations for background believability and storytelling, In *Proceedings of the 5th Workshop on Social Believability in Games*, August 1, 2016, Dundee, Scotland, UK: Abertay University.

Summerville, A.J., J. Ryan, M. Mateas, and N. Wardrip-Fruin, 2016, CFGs-2-NLU: Sequence-to-sequence learning for mapping utterances to semantics and pragmatics. Technical Report UCSC-SOE-16-11.

Team Bondi, 2011, *L.A. Noire*. New York: Rockstar Games.

Walsh, M., Modeling perception and awareness in Tom Clancy's Splinter Cell Blacklist, *Game AI Pro 2: Collected Wisdom of Game AI Professionals*, 313–326.

Welsh, R., 2013, Crytek's Target Tracks Perception System. *Game AI Pro: Collected Wisdom of Game AI Professionals*, 403:411.

Wilson, R.M., L.B. Gambrell, and W.R. Pfeiffer, 1985, The effects of retelling upon reading comprehension and recall of text information. *Journal of Educational Research*, 78(4):216–220.

Printed in the United States
by Baker & Taylor Publisher Services